Famous, not-so-famous or infamous, women in Bible times played an undeniable, significant role in the shaping of destiny. Some strove to be saint-like, to serve as the Master commanded. Others chose disobedience and sin. Many followed God one minute, looked back at the world—like Lot's wife—the next. They lived and loved, bore and raised children in a culture different from ours, a long-ago, faraway land we often consider primitive and unenlightened.

Were our sisters from the past really so different from we who live today? If they could step off the printed pages into our world, would they not surprise us, even teach us many things from the fire of their eternal womanhood?

Women of the Bible is a simple tribute to those whose stories are forever captured between the covers of the Holy Bible.

Women
of the
Bible

Colleen L. Reece is a popular and prolific writer of inspirational fiction, romance, and gift books. With over ninety books in print, Colleen's army of fans continues to grow. She loves to travel and at the same time do research for her many historical romances. Colleen resides in Auburn, Washington.

Women
of the
Bible

*Fifty Biographical Sketches
of Biblical Women*

Colleen L. Reece

A Barbour Book

ISBN 1-55748-817-7

Published by Barbour and Company, Inc.
P.O. Box 719
Uhrichsville, OH 44683

Printed in the United States of America

TABLE OF CONTENTS

OLD TESTAMENT

NEW TESTAMENT

The Gospels

Acts

EVE
GENESIS 2-4

Coolness patterned the garden into a mosaic of sunlight and shade. Soft footfalls announced the presence of One walking amidst trees and flowers. A voice, low but indescribably sweet, called, "Adam, where art thou?"

Trembling, the man and woman, formed and breathed into life by the Lord God Almighty, crept out of hiding. "Here, Lord," Adam whispered.

Eve shivered and clutched his arm, seeking strength yet knowing he had none to give the helpmeet God had created from one of Adam's ribs. The look in her husband's face when confronted by his Creator seared Eve's soul and burned like a hot coal that could not be extinguished. Fear. Shame. Regret. Brokenness. More than anything else, it showed her the magnitude of her folly. Why had she listened to the tempter? Worse, why had she caused her sinless husband to transgress God's law by encouraging him to do likewise?

If only they could go back just a few hours! The garden was beautiful. God said they might eat fruit from all the trees in the garden, save one. If they ate from that tree, they would surely die. Neither Eve nor Adam questioned God.

Then the serpent appeared. "Ye shall not die. God knows that in the day ye eat your eyes shall be opened. Ye shall be as gods, knowing good and evil."

The tree before Eve glowed with beauty, offering food alluring above all others—and something more: wisdom, as the serpent promised. She reached out, took fruit, and ate. How wonderful! She plucked more and ran with it to her husband, who accepted it from her hands.

Innocence vanished. Aware of their nakedness for the first time, they hastily gathered fig leaves and formed aprons to cover themselves. When they heard God walking in the garden, they fled. What had seemed such a little thing at the time turned monstrous in their new knowledge of good and evil.

Eve shuddered, sickened by how easily she had turned away from right and chosen wrong. Half-dazed, she heard Adam explaining to God that first Eve, then he, had eaten the forbidden fruit.

The Lord said to Eve. "What is this that thou hast done?"

Pierced to her innermost being by the sorrow in His voice, she said through dry lips, "The serpent beguiled me, and I did eat." Self-loathing filled her.

God cursed the serpent for what it had done. He condemned the tempter to crawl on its belly and said there would be enmity between him and womanhood forever. Then he turned back to Eve. "I will greatly multiply thy sorrow and thy conception; in sorrow thou shalt bring forth children; and thy desire shall be to thy husband, and he shall rule over thee."

Filled with misery and longing only to escape the presence of the One Who had made her, Eve suffered even more when the Lord spoke to Adam. Because he had listened to his wife rather than keep the commandment of God, he must toil all the days of his life. Thorns and thistles would hinder his work and only by the sweat of his brow would he be able to bring forth food from the ground now cursed.

God made coats of skins and clothed Adam and Eve. He drove them from the garden of Eden, lest they eat of the tree of life and live forever. Eve sobbed uncontrollably, but cherubim and a turning, flaming sword made it impossible for Adam and her to ever again walk with God in the garden.

Time passed. God's promises remained sure. Adam worked hard, tilling the ground. Eve brought forth children in travail, the mother of all living. Her heart tore with pain until she wondered if she would go mad when her eldest son Cain slew Abel, his younger brother, in a jealous rage.

Sorrow and joy, hard times and pleasant, the years rolled on. At times the lovely garden in which she and Adam had once walked with God seemed remote, shrouded by the mist of many years. Yet, as long as she lived, Eve never forgot her agony when she watched Adam face his Maker, and recognized what havoc she had brought into the world by listening to the tempter rather than to God.

SARAI
GENESIS 12, 16-18, 20-21, 23

Hunched and intense, Sarai listened to the remarkable tale her husband Abram related. "The Lord came to me in a vision. He told me He was my shield and my exceeding great reward. I cried to him, 'Lord, God, what will thou give me, seeing I go childless? Thou hast given me no seed, and lo, one born in my house is mine heir.'

"'This shall not be thine heir,' the Lord said. 'Look now toward heaven and tell the stars, if thou be able to number them. So shall thy seed be.'"

"You believe this to be true?" Sarai tried to keep her words calm, although her heart pounded with doubt.

"Yea, for He showed me many other things."

A ripple of scornful laughter escaped Sarai's lips. "I am an old woman, Abram," she proclaimed. "My child-bearing days—if I ever had such—are long past." Bitterness crept into her voice.

"I only know what the Lord has said." Abram rose and departed.

They spoke no more of the matter, but it lay between them, a living thing that permitted Sarai no rest. Why God had restrained her from bearing, she did not know. Why, then, had Jehovah given her husband the vision? Stay. Perhaps it was no vision but the product of Abram's longing for a son.

When Sarai could no longer bear the weight pressing on her she went to her husband. "Behold now, go in unto my maid; it may be that I may obtain children by her."

Abram hearkened to Sarai's voice. He took the Egyptian maid Hagar to be his wife and she conceived. At once, Hagar began to despise her mistress.

Sarai saw it. Fury raged within her. Had she not given Hagar to her own husband, that God's promise might be fulfilled? Now the younger woman dared set herself up against her mistress. It was unbearable.

"My wrong be upon thee," Sarai upbraided Abram. "I have given my maid into thy bosom and when she saw she had conceived, I was despised in her eyes: the Lord judge between me and thee." She held her breath, waiting his judgment.

"Behold, thy maid is in thy hand; do to her as it pleaseth thee."

Sarai dealt hardly with Hagar, who fled from her

wrath for a time.

When Abram was ninety and nine years old, the Lord appeared and gave him a new name: Abraham. He established an everlasting covenant to be God unto Abraham and his seed. He also gave Sarai a new name. Henceforth, she would be no longer Sarai but Sarah. She would have a son, who would be called Isaac, and become a mother of nations. Abraham fell upon his face and laughed in his heart. A man have a son at one hundred, with a wife of ninety long years? Never in the history of the world had such a thing happened.

Sarah could not and would not believe she would bear a son in her old age, but denied laughing for she was afraid. When she conceived and began to be great with child, Sarah pondered how such a thing could be. After long, empty years, God had granted her the desire of her heart.

Abraham was a hundred years old when Sarah delivered Isaac, whose name means "laughter." And she said, "God hath made me to laugh, so that all that hear will laugh with me. Who would have said unto Abraham that Sarah should have given children suck? For I have born him a son in his old age."

The child grew, and on the day Isaac was weaned, Abraham made a great feast. Sarah had not conquered her hatred of Hagar. She demanded that Hagar and her son Ishmael be cast out. Sarah rejoiced when the bond-woman and young Ishmael went away into the wilderness, not realizing God would one day make the young man ruler of a nation.

Sarah lived to be a hundred and twenty-seven years old. She never stopped marveling that God had sent a son into her barren life long after hope of such a thing had unfolded its wings and flown away.

HAGAR
GENESIS 16, 21

I hate being a handmaid, the Egyptian girl Hagar thought. *Especially for one like Sarai. She is old and ugly. I am younger and alive. Why must I serve and obey her?* She pressed her lips together, and her resentful thoughts rushed on. Nothing she did ever proved good enough for her fault-finding mistress. The plight of one who served had never weighed down on her so heavily as right now. Sarai became more demanding with each passing day.

Hagar smothered mirth, fearful of being discovered at the secret listening post where she learned much more than her mistress knew. Abram had just finished relating some impossible dream he called a vision from God.

Sarai's derisive laughter echoed in Hagar's heart. *The idea! What kind of God thought a man of Abram's age could father a child? Pah!* Her contempt grew. *Even if he were able, why would Sarai conceive now when she hadn't in all these years?* Hagar shook with silent laughter, but in the following days, she caught a brooding look in her mistress' eyes. She learned Sarai planned to give her handmaid to Abram.

At first the idea repelled Hagar, then cunning rose. A wife, even a second wife, held a more important place than a servant. Even though she never conceived, anything was better than her present position. She shrugged. Her wishes in the matter meant nothing. A handmaid did her mistress' bidding.

When Hagar knew she had conceived, triumph flooded through her. She made no attempt to hide her disdain of Sarai, childless and barren. As carrier of

Abram's son and heir, she felt she would also have his protection. She did not. He gave Sarai permission to deal with her as she would. Many a bitter tear Hagar wept before fleeing into the wilderness on the way to Shur. Not until she reached a fountain of water did she stop and wonder what would become of her and her unborn child. There an angel of the Lord found her.

"Whence camest thou? Whither wilt thou go?" he asked.

Rubbing her eyes to make sure she was not dreaming, Hagar replied, "I flee from the face of my mistress Sarai."

The angel told her she must return and submit herself to Sarai. He promised to multiply Hagar's seed exceedingly. He also told her she was with child and would bear a son. "The Lord has heard thy affliction," he said. "Name the child Ishmael"—whom God hears—"because the Lord hath heard thy affliction. And he will be a wild man; his hand against every man, and every man's hand against him."

Hagar returned to Sarai. Ishmael was born when Abram was fourscore and six years old. Abram's delight in his son made up for some of what Hagar suffered from Sarai, who daily grew more resentful of her handmaid and the boy. Things worsened when Ishmael was fourteen and Sarai, now Sarah, delivered Isaac. What would become of Hagar and Ishmael?

They soon found out. The next morning, Abraham, as he was called, rose early, put bread and a bottle of water on Hagar's shoulder and sent her away with Ishmael to wander in the wilderness of Beer-sheba.

When the water was spent, she cast her son under one of the shrubs and went a far distance off. "Let me not see the death of the child." She lifted up her voice and wept.

The angel of God called to Hagar out of heaven. "What aileth thee, Hagar? fear not; for God hath heard the voice of the lad. Arise, lift up the lad, and hold him in thy hand; for I will make him a great nation." God opened Hagar's eyes and she saw a well of water. She filled the bottle and gave the lad drink, holding the promises of the angel of God deep in her heart.

As Ishmael grew, God was with him. The boy dwelt in the wilderness and became an archer. Hagar took him a wife out of the land of Egypt and great was her joy. Outcasts from the tents of Abraham they might be, yet God had protected her and the child of her body. Twice an angel had promised Ishmael would be a great nation. One day it would come to pass. Blessed be Jehovah!

LOT'S WIFE
GENESIS 19

Lot, brother of Abraham, hastened home at eventide and called to his wife, "Make haste! Prepare unleavened bread."

The mistress of the household looked up, startled by his excitement. She caught sight of two strangers entering the house behind him. "Who—?"

Lot lowered his voice. "As I sat at the gate of the city, two angels came to me. I bowed and prayed that they might tarry all night in this, their servant's house. At first they said nay, they would abide in the street, but when I pressed upon them greatly, they agreed."

Angels! The woman's mouth fell open, but she hurried to do her husband's bidding, pressing her daughters into service, as well.

Before the household lay down for the night, the men of Sodom encircled the dwelling place, demanding the strangers be brought to them.

Lot stepped outside and closed the door. He entreated them not to do wickedly. He said, "Behold, I have two daughters which have not known man; let me, I pray you, bring them out unto you, and do ye to them as is good in your eyes: only unto these men do nothing; for therefore came they under the shadow of my roof."

Anger raged inside his listening wife. Was he insane to sacrifice his own daughters for the sake of the two sheltered under his roof? If they were indeed angels, could they not protect themselves from the rabble outside the door?

Lot's pleas proved useless. The crowd pressed sore upon Lot and came forth to break the door. Before they could do so, the strangers pulled Lot inside, shut the door, and smote the mob with such blindness they could not find the door.

Weak with relief, Lot's wife sank back to her pallet and clutched a shawl around her. She heard the visitors say, "Hast thou here any besides? son-in-law, and thy sons, and thy daughters, and whatsoever thou hast in the city, bring them out of this place; for we will destroy this, because the cry of them is grown great before the face of the Lord; and the Lord hath sent us to destroy it."

Destroy the city? The listening woman plucked at her shawl with nerveless fingers. Lot went out and told his sons-in-law they must get up and leave at once. They laughed and mocked him, refusing to believe the Lord would destroy the city.

In the morning the angels hastened Lot. "Arise, take thy wife, and thy two daughters which are here; lest they be consumed in the iniquity of the city." While Lot lingered, the angels laid hold upon his hand, and his wife and daughters' hands, and led them forth, the Lord being merciful. One angel warned, "Escape for thy life; look not behind thee, neither stay thou in all the plain; escape to the mountain, lest thou be consumed."

Lot pleaded that they might instead flee to a little city and that it would not be overthrown. The angel agreed, and again urged them to make haste.

The sun had risen by the time Lot and his wife entered Zoar. Terrible sounds came from Sodom and Gomorrah, even from the plain and all that grew on the ground. Lot's wife could not stand it. From her position behind her husband, she wailed with grief. Only two of her daughters had been saved. The others had remained in Sodom with their husbands. In her despair, she turned her face toward the way they had come, either ignoring or forgetting the commandment the angel had given not to look back. Fire and brimstone fell from heaven, devouring everything and everyone in its path.

When Lot and his daughters sought the wife and mother who had accompanied them, nothing remained but a pillar of salt.

REBEKAH
GENESIS 24, 27

The eldest servant of the house of Abraham knelt by a well of water near the city of Nahor in Mesopotamia. Ten laden camels waited nearby. "Oh Lord God of my master, Abraham, I pray thee, send me good speed this day, and show kindness unto my master." He paused. Could he fulfill the oath he had made to his master? Abraham had told him an angel would go before and lead the trusted servant to a kinswoman willing to accompany him to the tents of Abraham and become wife to Abraham's son Isaac. How would a humble servant know her?

He continued, "Behold, I stand here by the well. The daughters of the men of the city come out to draw water. Let it come to pass that the damsel to whom I shall say, 'Let down thy pitcher, that I may drink'; and she shall say, 'Drink, and I will give thy camels drink also': let the same be she that thou hast appointed for thy servant Isaac."

Before he had finished speaking, Rebekah, a fair young virgin, went down to the well and filled her pitcher. She curiously eyed the stranger and his well-laden camels. He asked for water and she gladly gave him her brimming pitcher. "I will also draw water for the camels," she told the stranger. Pitcher after pitcher she drew and poured into the trough so the camels could quench their thirst.

When they finished, the servant gave Rebekah a golden earring of half a shekel weight, two bracelets, and ten shekels' weight of gold. He asked her father's name and if lodging could be had in his house.

"I am daughter of Bethuel, the son of Milcah, which she bare unto Nahor," she proudly announced. "We have both straw and provender enough, and room to lodge in."

Nahor, brother of Abraham! The servant bowed his head and worshipped the Lord, praising Him for His leading.

Rebekah ran and told those of her household concerning the strange encounter. Her brother Laban immediately went for the stranger and welcomed him. While they sat at meat, the servant told everything that had transpired. He told how rich Abraham was in flocks and herds, of servants, silver, gold, and beasts. He related how a son had been born to Sarah in her old age and that Abraham had sent his eldest servant to find a kinswoman to become Isaac's wife.

Rebekah's heart leaped within her, especially when the man confessed he had prayed for God to lead the right woman to the well and had even given the words she should say! Humility at having been selected by God as Isaac's wife filled her and she breathlessly waited for her family to speak.

"Wilt thou go with this man?" Laban and Bethuel asked Rebekah.

"I will." They blessed her and sent her on her journey.

Rebekah whiled away the weary traveling hours wondering what her husband-to-be would be like. When she first saw Isaac, she found him pleasant to look upon. His eyes held love, and she became his wife.

Twenty barren years later, when Isaac was three score, the Lord blessed Rebekah with twins: Esau, hairy and red, then Jacob. Esau turned to hunting and the field, and Jacob, whom Rebekah loved more, dwelt in the tents. She secretly rejoiced when Esau sold his birthright to his younger brother for bread and a pottage of lentils. Had not Jacob been born with one hand on Esau's heel, symbolizing that he, not his elder brother, should rule?

Isaac grew old. Rebekah's ambitions for Jacob soared. She commanded him to disguise himself as Esau, present the savory meat Isaac loved, and receive the blessing that belonged to the older son. Fear soon replaced her joy. The cheated Esau threatened to kill Jacob, and Rebekah sent her favorite son away, weeping bitterly.

What had she done? What good was her life if Jacob chose the wrong woman for his wife? She took comfort when Isaac charged Jacob to pass by the daughters of Canaan, go to Rebekah's father, and take a wife from among the daughters of Laban, her brother. Yet again and again she remembered the bitter enmity she had sown between her sons because of her terrible desire for Jacob to rule.

RACHEL
GENESIS 29-31, 35

Of the many tasks necessary to keep her father's household and holdings running smoothly, his younger daughter Rachel best liked caring for the sheep. Sometimes her older sister Leah chided her about it. "Why can't you be like other women, instead of always wanting to be off with a smelly bunch of animals?" She pulled a long face. "You won't see me chasing after unruly lambs or rams and ewes that have to be pulled from thickets." Leah delicately pinched her nostrils with a thumb and forefinger. "No man will seek your hand when you smell like dirty, wet wool."

Rachel only laughed. What cared she? Still young in years, she had plenty of time to find a husband. She refrained from saying so. For some reason, Leah had waited year after year for love to seek her out, but remained unbetrothed. Rachel loved her sister and could not understand why men passed Leah by. Perhaps if she hadn't been so busy tending sheep, Rachel would have spent more time peering into a pool of water, noticing the reflection of a beautiful, well-favored young woman—whose charms made Leah's tender eyes pale into insignificance by comparison.

One day Rachel and her flocks came to a well in the field, as was her custom. A great stone lay rolled in the well's mouth. When all the flocks of sheep were gathered, the stone was rolled away and the shepherds watered the sheep. This day a strange young man stood nearby. Rachel hesitated, feeling hot color steal into her smooth cheeks and not knowing why.

To her surprise, he came straight to her. "You are the daughter of Laban, son of Nahor?"

"Why—yes. I am Rachel." Her heart pounded.

"I have traveled far. I am your kinsman Jacob, son of Isaac who married Rebekah, sister of Laban." He kissed Rachel, lifted up his voice, and wept.

Rachel broke free, stared, then ran to tell her father. More than the exertion of running made her heart beat more wildly than ever. That unruly member continued to leap in the most unmaidenly way all through the month

Jacob abode with Laban and his family. Rachel hid it as best she could and refused to even discuss Jacob with Leah.

At the end of the month, Jacob struck a bargain with Laban. "Rachel has found favor in my sight. I will serve thee seven years for her hand."

Laban saw the chance to gain an expert workman. "It is better that I give her to thee than to another man: abide with me."

For seven years, Jacob served Laban, never suspecting the scheme in the other's cunning mind. When the marriage feast finally came, Laban exchanged Leah for Rachel. The next day, Jacob bitterly accused him of treachery. Laban replied that in their country the firstborn must wed before the younger. "You shall also have Rachel if you vow to serve seven more years," he promised.

Rachel, who had been distraught at her sister's marriage to Jacob, felt hope stir in her heart. Yet it seemed much to ask. Fourteen years, for the love of a maiden? Such a thing had never before been done in her country.

"I will serve," Jacob huskily told Laban, gaze steady on Rachel. Nothing could have showed Rachel better how much she was loved—far more than her sister Leah ever could be. It sustained her through the years when Leah bore strong sons and a daughter, but Rachel remained barren.

But God had not forgotten Rachel. Finally, she conceived and bore a son. She praised the Lord, crying, "God hath taken away my reproach." She called her son Joseph, meaning "He shall add." She also said, "The Lord shall add to me another son," and kept the foreknowledge close in her heart.

Rachel died birthing Benjamin, her second son, and was buried on the way to Bethlehem. Her name lives on as a mother in Israel who loved her husband, her children, and her God.

LEAH
GENESIS 29-31

Leah, daughter of Laban, hated the elder-sister role life had forced her to play. Why must a woman with a loving heart be condemned to idleness simply because no man had yet spoken for her? Must she forever be compared with another, always unfavorably?

Leah loved Rachel. Sometimes she exulted in the girl's young beauty. More often she despaired. In her deepest soul-searching, she honestly admitted it was unreasonable to believe anyone would pass fair Rachel by in favor of the elder sister. Her lip curled. The few who had, had done so with an eye to Laban's holdings, not for love of his daughter. She would have none of them.

The day their kinsman Jacob came, Leah felt a stirring deep inside. Here was a man who more than fulfilled her secret dreams. Strong, gentle, his very presence made Leah's heart throb with longing, then grow numb at the look in his eyes. There was no room in his heart for anyone but Rachel.

In spite of the knowledge, Leah refused to accept defeat. Had she not seven years to show herself as worthy as Rachel, if not as beautiful? Even when months fled into years and the marriage feast day drew near, a slim hope remained. Would Laban, powerful as he was, break tradition and allow his younger daughter to wed first?

In a twinkling, everything changed. Leah could scarcely grasp the rapid change in her life. She, not Rachel, became Jacob's wife. Triumph blotted out all else—until the next morning. Hope of his loving her vanished when Jacob discovered Laban's deceit. Leah wondered if she would ever forget the sight of his face when he beheld her, not Rachel, for whom he had toiled so long. Like a slim, keen blade, it plunged into her heart, twisting and turning when her father extracted Jacob's vow to serve another seven years in exchange for Rachel. Now she lay sleepless, passionately wishing her husband lay by her side and not her sister's. She could imagine them whispering, perhaps blaming her as well as Laban. At times she writhed, wishing she had never seen the man who had become her husband, then passionately clutching at the shreds of his love with both hands in an attempt to convince herself one day he would care.

When the Lord saw Leah was not loved, He blessed her with children. With each child, she felt Jacob must surely learn to love her, especially when her sister remained barren. Instead, Jacob's heart lingered with Rachel, his first and only real love. Six strong sons and one beautiful daughter Leah gave her husband, rejoicing in each, clinging to the fading vision of one day possessing Jacob's heart.

After the birth of Dinah, God hearkened unto Rachel and she conceived. Jacob's countenance wore joy far beyond any he had ever shown over the arrival of a child by Leah. Again hurt flayed his first wife.

Leah faced greater conflict once Rachel delivered her

son Benjamin. Jacob, now called Israel, could not hide the fact he cared far more for Joseph and Benjamin, Rachel's sons, than his other sons and daughter.

Though she desperately tried, Leah never recaptured the brief triumph she had known on her marriage day. As in girlhood, her fair young sister's shadow lay over Leah all the days of her life.

POTIPHAR'S WIFE
GENESIS 39

Potiphar's wife eyed the well-favored young slave her Egyptian husband had acquired some time before. A slow smile crept over her painted lips. What an open-faced youngster this Joseph was! Her sluggish blood, jaded by many conquests, stirred. Young men always attracted her. She licked her lips like a giant cat savoring its prey long before securing it.

"Where did you find him?" she asked.

Potiphar, captain of the guard and highly respected, smiled at her. No one dared inform him of his wife's indiscretions. To do so meant risking terrible punishment. Even if one spoke, Potiphar would not believe. His fierce, possessive love blinded him to the wickedness thinly veiled to all but him.

"An interesting story." He glanced at Joseph and paused. The woman reclining on a couch saw a flicker of pain in the young slave's face. "You may go," Potiphar told Joseph, who gracefully walked away. It brought another gleam to the wife's eyes.

"He seems—healthy."

"He's far more than that. He has served so well I have put him in charge of all my affairs. Never have I had such an overseer." A strange look crossed Potiphar's face. "Since he took charge, my holdings have increased." He laughed. "Joseph says his God has blessed this house and my fields."

"His god!" A quick swing of her feet brought the woman to a sitting position. "Which one? Osiris, god of the underworld?"

Potiphar shook his head. "No. Joseph worships one he calls Jehovah. He says there are no other gods. Anyway, the boy was born to his father's favorite wife in later years. The old man loved Joseph more than his half-brothers and made him a coat of many colors. It made the others hate him. Things worsened when Joseph told of a dream that when interpreted meant he would rule over his family and they would one day bow down to him."

"I should think it would!" Interest whetted, Potiphar's wife disdainfully flicked a hand. If she chose to pursue her interest in the young man, he needn't think she would bow to him—or any other.

"Most of the brothers wanted to kill him but Reuben, the eldest, intervened. He convinced them to shed no blood but cast the boy into a pit. Later they sold him to a band of Ishmaelites who brought him to Egypt. A good day for us," he added.

"A good day," she agreed, fingers stroking her silken draperies.

Potiphar's wife bided her time, taking care to act circumspectly in front of her husband but casting meaningful glances toward Joseph on every possible occasion. He seemed not to see them. It baffled her. Was he so innocent he could not see her invitation? Or so clever he chose to ignore it? The thought sent scarlet flags to her cheeks.

One day when Potiphar was not home, his wife summoned Joseph and sent away her maids. Her heart raced with excitement. "Come." She gestured to the couch where she lay.

Joseph refused, saying he could sin neither against his master nor his God.

Potiphar's wife hid her rage and shrugged. He would lay aside his scruples soon enough. Yet time after time, Joseph continued to refuse her advances. His reluctance goaded her on until she determined to break his will.

One afternoon when no other men were in the house, Joseph once more turned down her invitation. She snatched his garment. He fled, leaving it in her hand. Enraged at being rejected, she cried in a loud voice, "See? the Hebrew came in to mock me. When I cried out, he fled, leaving his garment." She told the same tale to her husband when he came home. None of the household dared deny her lies.

Potiphar's wrath kindled against the young man he had trusted with all he possessed. He comforted his sobbing wife and had Joseph thrown into prison. He never knew his wife rejoiced—then decked herself out for her next conquest.

JOCHEBED
EXODUS 2

Strange thoughts troubled the king of Egypt. He was new to the throne, and his perplexities rose daily.

Some he could shunt off to his advisors but not the ever-growing problem he encountered each time he gazed on his subjects. The children of Israel who dwelt in the land were fruitful. They increased abundantly. They multiplied and waxed exceeding mighty until the land was filled with them. He abominated them all and, worse, feared what they might become and do.

The king said to his people, "Behold, the people of the children of Israel are more and mightier than we. We must deal wisely with them. If war should come they would join our enemies, and fight against us, and so get them up out of the land." The corners of his mouth drew down and he swished his royal robes.

At the king's orders, taskmasters were appointed to afflict the children of Israel with their burdens. They were held in bitter bondage and forced to build for Pharaoh treasure cities, Pithom and Raamses. In mortar and brick and all manner of service of the fields they were made to serve, to endure the hardship or drop and be beaten. Death offered the only freedom. For four hundred years, they were enslaved. Yet the more the Egyptians afflicted them, the more the Israelites multiplied and grew.

Could nothing stop them? The king ordered the Hebrew midwives to perform a terrible task. At the time of delivery, daughters might live; every son must be killed. The midwives feared God. They saved the men children alive, in spite of their orders to the contrary.

The king called for them and demanded, "Why have ye done this thing?"

The midwives said unto Pharaoh, "The Hebrew women are lively, not like the Egyptian women. They are delivered ere we come in unto them." God dealt well with the midwives and the people continued to multiply and wax mighty.

Determined not to be outwitted, Pharaoh charged all his people, saying, "Every son that is born ye shall cast into the river, and every daughter ye shall save alive." A wailing in Egypt rose that assaulted the ears of its inhabitants as the dark river waters swallowed up countless innocent male children.

About this time, a daughter of the house of Levi, married to Amram, also of the house of Levi, conceived. Jochebed bore a son. She refused to comply with the king's edict, believing somehow the child must be saved. For three terrifying months she concealed her child, but the time came when she could no longer keep him without discovery.

"I cannot let my baby be destroyed," she whispered into the shawl that held him. A plan born of desperation formed. She made an ark of bulrushes, a floating basket daubed with slime and pitch to keep the water out. Jochebed carefully tucked the child in its depths, covered him, and eased it in the flags by the brink of the river that had claimed the lives of so many other babies.

Why must such things be? her aching heart silently cried. Then, *Lord God of Israel, protect my little son.*

"Stay hidden by the river," Jochebed commanded her daughter Miriam. "Watch the ark carefully. We must know what happens to this, thy brother." She stumbled away, knowing she had done all she could to save her child but wondering how she could stand the pain.

Some time later, her daughter Miriam rushed home. "Mother, Mother!" Her childish, treble voice rose to a high, excited pitch. "Pharaoh's daughter found the ark." She stopped for breath. "You are to nurse the baby—for wages!"

Never in her wildest imaginations had Jochebed envisioned such an outcome. The best she had hoped was for a kindly soul to rescue the child and conceal it as she could no longer do. Jochebed fell to her knees. "Blessed be the Lord God of Israel," she cried. "Jehovah has heard my prayer and this day delivered my son by His mighty hand." A little later, she settled down, nursing the son doomed to die by Pharaoh's decree but spared by God for a mighty, world-changing role.

MIRIAM
EXODUS 2, 15; NUMBERS 12

S mall Miriam carefully held the tiny bundle her mother had placed in her eager arms. Eyes round, she touched the miniature fingers, and gently stroked the baby's soft cheek. "Mother, he is so beautiful. Surely God will not allow him to die." She hopefully looked up at Jochebed, busy with bulrushes, slime and pitch.

Her mother sighed. "I hope not, child. Yet other beautiful children have died by order of the wicked Pharaoh. If only we could leave this land of bondage! How long, oh, Lord, how long?"

The familiar cry for freedom, kept low to keep from disturbing the sleeping baby, rang loud in Miriam's ears. Child that she was, she yet recognized the longing. It echoed in her heart. "If we are Jehovah's chosen people, why does He allow us to be oppressed?" she fiercely demanded.

"Hush, Miriam. It is not for us to question the ways

of Jehovah. Besides—" Jochebed's nimble fingers stilled and a faraway look came to her eyes. She lowered her voice to a whisper and her daughter leaned closer. Even walls had ears these days. No one knew how idle words crept into the wind but speaking of certain subjects meant harsh punishments, even death.

"My child, one day a deliverer will be sent, one to lead God's people out of this land and into a place of freedom."

A deliverer. In a passion she could not describe, Miriam fiercely whispered, "When will the deliverer come?" Her gaze dropped to the little brother she loved with all the feelings of her young heart. "Mother, why does Jehovah not send the deliverer now, when we need him so badly?"

"We cannot know the ways of the Lord," Jochebed sadly told her. She continued smearing the ark with slime and pitch. "There, it is finished. When it dries, it will be the finest small boat anyone could ask. We shall pray for it to safely carry your brother to someone who will care for him."

A little later, Miriam watched her mother place the baby in his new floating cradle. Awake now, he made no cry. Jochebed laid the ark on the water, admonished her daughter to keep watch, and trudged away.

For a time nothing happened. Then a rustle warned Miriam someone approached. She made herself small in her hiding place.

"Why, what is that?" someone said.

Miriam gasped and peeked from shelter. The Pharaoh's daughter stood a short distance away. Her maid drew the basket with the baby from the water. The compassion in the look Pharaoh's daughter bestowed on the crying baby gave Miriam courage to spring forth and ask if she should bring a Hebrew nurse for the child. On winged, bare feet, she sped to her mother with the gladsome news.

Miriam became a fine woman, respected by her people. She served as a prophetess, skilled with timbrel playing and dancing, singing praises to the Lord, and rejoicing over the goodness of God. Yet in spite of her calling, she at one time allowed jealousy to influence her and spoke against Moses for marrying an Ethopian woman. "Hath the Lord spoken only by Moses?" she and Aaron demanded. "Hath He not also spoken by us?"

A strangled cry arose from Moses and Aaron. They speechlessly pointed.

Miriam looked down at her hands and tottered. Her skin had turned white as snow from leprosy. "Oh, God, what have I done?" she wailed.

Moses cried to the Lord on her behalf, imploring Him to remove the curse. The Lord in His goodness hearkened unto Moses' pleadings, but for seven long days Miriam was shut out of the camp for her rebelliousness. After she rejoined the others, she again became respected and never tired of telling how Jehovah had saved Moses, the deliverer who freed the Israelite people from Pharaoh's cruel hand and led them to the Promised Land.

PHARAOH'S DAUGHTER
EXODUS 2

In the eyes of those who dwelt in Egypt, Pharaoh's daughter had everything a girl or woman could desire. The finest silks and cloth of gold clothed her. Jewels lay unworn in costly caskets, simply because of their number. The very stars in the heavens could not outshine Pharaoh's daughter when her maidens decked her out.

Only one thing did she not have: peace of mind. Naturally compassionate and kind-hearted, she raged when her father the king ordered the Hebrew midwives Shiphrah and Puah to kill all sons of the Hebrew children when they were called to serve in their office. She secretly rejoiced when the midwives did not obey the commandment. How clever of them to say the Hebrew women were more lively than those of Egypt and had already delivered the children by the time the midwives came!

One day the daughter of Pharaoh went to the special place in the river where she washed herself. She walked along the river's side, anticipating the clean, fresh coolness awaiting in the secluded spot she had made her own. Yet today a foreign presence had entered her domain. Something rocked among the flags.

"Bring it to me that I might behold it," Pharaoh's daughter ordered her maid. The servant obeyed. Pharaoh's daughter bent low over the retrieved object. "Why, it's an ark, fashioned of bulrushes, daubed with slime and pitch! How came such a thing to my bathing place?"

Nimble fingers opened the ark. Pharaoh's daughter's eyes grew wide at sight of the contents. A tiny wail issued from the basket. Fear clutched the girl's heart. She sent a hasty glance back toward her maidens. "Be gone! I will remain here for a time."

Giggling and fluttering, they hastened to obey. When only her maid remained, Pharaoh's daughter drew forth the babe. Compassion filled her soul. "This is one of the Hebrews' children." Color fled from her face. "What shall we do? If Father knows the small one lives, he will order the babe thrown into the river, as so many before him. His life will be snuffed out like a candle in the wind." She held the tiny boy close to her beating heart and he nestled against her. "It shall not be! He is mine."

A small voice beside her whispered, "Shall I go and call to thee a nurse of the Hebrew women, that she may nurse the child for thee?"

Pharaoh's daughter whirled, the babe still clutched close to her bosom. Liquid brown eyes stared out of a smooth face. Something in their depths silently assured Pharaoh's daughter she had nothing to fear from the Hebrew girl-child before her. "Go," she commanded.

With fast-beating heart, she waited the short time that felt like hours. The Hebrew child returned, holding an older woman by the hand. The suffering of the Israelite people shone in the woman's eyes, but her gaze met Pharaoh's daughter honestly. Again came a feeling of trust. "Take this child away and nurse it for me, and I will give thee wages," Pharaoh's daughter ordered. She noted the way the woman's gentle hands accepted the wrapped babe, the instinctive cuddling that came only from a woman who possessed great love for all children.

"His name is Moses," Pharaoh's daughter said. "For I drew him from the water. He shall be my son."

Level gaze met level gaze. The woman smiled and bowed. A strange, mystical expression crept into her eyes. "It is well." She bowed again and walked away with her charge.

Pharaoh's daughter stared after her, wondering. The Hebrew nurse's face had filled with such radiance that in spite of her rude clothing, she appeared lovelier by far than the Pharaoh's daughter in all her glory.

ZIPPORAH

EXODUS 2, 18

Reuel, the priest of Midian (also called Jethro) had seven daughters. Zipporah, "the bird," was one of them. A maiden's life in the land of Midian was not easy. Time after time when the girls came to the well to draw water, fill the troughs, and water their father's flocks, unfriendly shepherds drove them away, mocking, laughing, and calling out crude jests. Even Zipporah, strong and unafraid, could not stand against them. They were forced to wait long before watering the sheep.

One day Reuel's daughters came home to their father, driving their flocks and arriving far earlier than was their custom.

"How is it that ye are come so soon today?" he inquired.

A babble of voices arose, excited and incoherent.

"Silence!" their father commanded. "Speak one at a time so a man can comprehend what it is you wish to convey."

His daughters obeyed, but eyes and faces shone with the startling occurrence that had taken place earlier in the day.

"We took the flock to the well for water," one began.

"The shepherds came as usual to drive us away," another said.

"Suddenly an Egyptian came, we know not from whence." The story grew even more amazing. "He dealt hardly with the shepherds and delivered us out of their hands,"

"That isn't all," several chorused.

One added, "The stranger also drew water enough for us and watered the flock that we might not have it to do."

Reuel marveled and said unto his daughters, "Where is he? Why is it that ye have left the man? Call him, that he may eat bread."

Weary from his long journey, sick at heart over having slain an Egyptian he'd found smiting his Israelite brethren, Moses gladly accepted the kindly priest's offer of shelter and sustenance. He had left Egypt after one Hebrew who strove with another asked, "Who made thee a judge over us? Intendest thou to kill me, as thou killedst the Egyptian?" At that moment, Moses had realized his deed was known and he was in great danger from Pharaoh. Here in Midian he could abide in content.

Zipporah looked on Moses with favor. Unlike the men of her own country, his deep gaze sent warmth to her skin and longing to her heart. The day her father gave her to be Moses' wife brought joy beyond belief. So did the birth of their son. Moses insisted the child be called Gershom and said, "I have been a stranger in a strange land."

Zipporah tried hard to understand the things her husband told her. Still she wondered. What manner of man saw burning bushes that were not consumed? And talked with Jehovah, as a man to a friend?

Greater questions were yet to come, then a long separation. After traveling with her husband to Egypt, where his brethren were enslaved, Zipporah's heart ached when Moses sent her back to her father in Midian to wait there with their sons Gershom and Eliezer. Tales came to them of the many plagues visited on the Egyptians because of the hardness of Pharaoh's heart and of the release of the Israelites after the death of the Egyptians' firstborn. More stories rode the wind: the parting of a sea to provide dry land on which Moses and his followers trod. Once they were safe, the rush of water that drowned the attacking Egyptian army. The children of Israel being fed manna in the wilderness.

At times Zipporah wondered if she would ever again cast her gaze on the man who had captured her love but held true to a higher calling. At last, great happiness came. Jethro heard of what God had done for Moses. He took Zipporah, Gershom, and Eliezer and came to the tents of Moses in the wilderness. Jethro rejoiced for the goodness the Lord had done and said, "Now I know the Lord is greater than all gods: for in the thing wherein they dealt proudly he was above them." Zipporah's joy knew no bounds—and she marveled at what a mighty leader her husband Moses had become.

RAHAB
JOSHUA 2, 6

Rahab, harlot and innkeeper, stared into the faces of the two strangers who had taken lodging in her house. What manner of men were they, these bold Israelites who dared enter Jericho? As she spoke with them, the tittle-tattle that had raced through the streets of Jericho and into every house kept time with their story. A strange and unexplainable feeling came, an assurance that all who had heard of the protecting hand of the Lord Who watched over His chosen people was true. Yet what had she to do with the matter? The men had obviously come to spy out the land, with full intentions of making it their own. Even now the king's soldiers would be seeking the Israelites.

Rahab scarcely believed her own ears when she whispered, "Come!" Heart beating wildly, she led them to the roof of the house. She hid them under stalks of flax, laid in order on the roof. "Do not make a sound or you will surely be discovered," she ordered them. "If you are, you not only bring death to yourselves, but to all of the house of Rahab." She slipped away.

A loud pounding on the door sent blood hurrying through her veins. She flung it open. "What do you want?" she demanded of the king's soldiers.

"In the name of the king, bring forth the men that are come to thee," came the reply. "It has been told to the king of Jericho they are children of Israel, come to search out the country."

Rahab didn't betray herself by even the blink of an eyelash. "There came men to me, but I wist not whence they were; it came to pass that the men went out, about the time of the shutting of the gate when darkness fell. Pursue them quickly; for ye shall overtake them."

The king's men eyed her suspiciously; Rahab's steady glance did not waver. She stood in the doorway until certain they had gone, then waited a time to make sure none lurked behind to see if she spoke the truth.

When all grew still, Rahab went back to the roof. She told the spies, "I know the Lord hath given you the land. Your terror is fallen upon us, and all the inhabitants of the land faint because of you. When we heard how the Lord dried up the water of the Red Sea for you when you came out of Egypt, our hearts did melt, neither did there remain any more courage in any man, because of you: for the Lord your God is God in heaven above, and in earth beneath." She paused, hands clenched and wet with sweat.

"I pray you, swear unto me by the Lord, since I have showed you kindness, that you will also show kindness unto my father's house, and give me a true token. . .save alive my father, and my mother, and my brethren, and my sisters, and all that they have, and deliver our lives from death."

The Israelites exchanged glances. They promised Rahab if she kept silent about the whole business, when the Lord gave them the land, they would deal kindly and truly with her.

Great relief filled her. "Come." She took them to the window and let them down by a cord, for her house was upon the town wall, but not before they bade her bind a line of scarlet thread in the same window and bring her family and all their household inside the inn. Whosoever went outside would die. All who remained inside the house with the scarlet thread would be spared.

Rahab did as commanded. When the walls of Jericho fell before Joshua and his men, only Rahab and those with her in the house did not perish. The two young spies she had saved took her and her kindred to the camp of Israel. Her heart burned within her. One act of kindness had brought mercy for those she loved.

The genealogy of Christ given in Matthew 1 lists Rahab as the mother of Boaz, great-grandfather of King David. If this is she who saved Joshua's men, it seems likely Rahab turned from her wickedness and sought forgiveness from the Lord she recognized as God of heaven and earth.

DEBORAH
JUDGES 4-5

Deborah, prophetess and judge of Israel, dwelt beneath her palm tree between Ramah and Bethel. The children of Israel came to her for judgments in disputes they either could not or would not settle on their own. Sometimes Lapidoth, her husband, felt they taxed his wife beyond measure, yet he took great pride in the wisdom of her decisions. Did not all who knew Deborah love and respect her for the high position to which Jehovah had called her?

Not all of Deborah's troubles came from those she served. The Lord had also burdened her concerning her people. War with Sisera, captain of King Jabin's army, loomed as inevitable. Anticipation of the forthcoming battle lay on Deborah's heart like a heavy stone.

One day she called Barak, son of Abinoam out of Kedesh-naphtali, and demanded, "Has the Lord God of Israel not commanded us to go and draw toward Mount Tabor, taking ten thousand men of the children of Naphtali and Zebulun? Jehovah Himself has promised to draw Sisera with his chariots and multitude to the river Kishon and deliver him into our hand."

Barak, resembling the thunderbolt and lightning for which he had been named, flung his head back. "If you will go with me, I will go. If you will not, then I will not go."

Deborah faced him squarely. A dozen thoughts chased through her active brain. *A woman in battle, leading against the foe? Such a thing had never been heard of. What would those she judged think of her? Why not?* she silently asked herself. *Had not God called her first as a prophetess, then as a judge?* "I will go, notwithstanding the journey you take shall not be for your honor. The Lord shall sell Sisera into the hand of a woman."

Barak agreed, and Deborah arose straightway and went with him to Kedesh, where Zebulun and Naphtali awaited them, in answer to Barak's call. Ten thousand men responded and accompanied Barak and Deborah.

On the morning of the battle, Deborah said unto Barak, "Up, for this is the day in which the Lord has delivered Sisera into thine hand."

When Sisera heard that Barak had gone up to Mount Tabor, he gathered together his nine hundred chariots of iron and a multitude of warriors. A terrible battle ensued, but the Lord discomfited Sisera, his chariots, and all his host. When the battle ended, not an enemy remained alive.

Deborah and Barak joined in a song of praise, thanking God for delivering the foes into their hands. They spoke of how God sent a mother in Israel to defeat those who had chosen new gods. They named those who had joined Deborah and Barak in the fray: the princes of Issachar as well as kings who came and fought without gain of money. They sang, "They fought from heaven; the stars in their courses fought against Sisera."

At last, the ceaseless pounding in Deborah's soul stilled. The land had rest forty years. The name of Deborah took its place in history as one who first judged, then led her people both wisely and well.

SAMSON'S MOTHER
JUDGES 13-15

A certain man named Manoah, whose wife was barren, lived in the midst of the children of Israel, who again did evil in the sight of the Lord and were delivered into the hand of the Philistines for forty years.

One day an angel of the Lord appeared unto the woman and said unto her, "Behold now, thou art barren, and bearest not: but thou shalt conceive, and bear a son. Now therefore beware, I pray thee, and drink not wine nor strong drink, and eat not any unclean thing: For, lo, thou shalt conceive, and bear a son; and no razor shall come on his head: for the child shall be a Nazarite unto God from the womb: and he shall begin to deliver Israel out of the hand of the Philistines."

Manoah's wife rejoiced greatly and ran to tell her husband. "A man of God came unto me, and his countenance was like the countenance of an angel of God, very terrible: but I asked him not whence he was, neither told he me his name." She faithfully related the rest of the angel's message.

Manoah, much impressed, entreated the Lord, asking for the man of God to come again and teach them what they should do unto the child that would be born. God heard the prayer. The angel came to the woman in the field. She made haste and brought Manoah to him. The angel repeated the instructions he had given earlier but refused to eat bread with them. Manoah took a kid and made an offering. When the flame rose, the angel of the Lord ascended in the flame of the altar. Manoah and his wife looked on it, and fell on their faces to the ground.

"We shall surely die," Manoah wailed. "We have seen God."

His wife reminded him God would not have showed them all the things if He planned to kill them. She kept that hope in her heart and one day bore a son. "He shall be called Samson, which means like the sun," she told her husband.

The child grew and the Lord blessed him. When Samson became a young man, a daughter of the Philistines found favor in his eyes. His mother's heart quailed within her. She and Manoah protested, "Is there not a woman among the daughters of thy brethren, or among all my people, that thou goest to take a wife of the uncircumcised Philistines?"

Samson insisted they get her for him, for she pleased him well. Sad-hearted, his mother traveled with her husband and son to the vineyards of Timnath. There a young lion roared against Samson. The Spirit of the Lord came so mightily upon the young man, he killed the lion—but he did not tell his father or mother. Still, they realized their son had been set apart before his birth to do great things.

Samson's mother kept her counsel. The father made a contract with the woman their son desired, and Samson held a great feast. Strong, untamed, and uncut hair hanging over his mighty shoulders, he sent a thrill of pride through his mother, although her woman's heart feared for him because he had chosen a Philistine's daughter to wed.

Her fears proved well-grounded. Men at the feast threatened to burn the bride and her father's house if she did not entice Samson to give her the answer to a riddle he had posed. If they could declare the answer in the seven days of the feast, they would receive thirty sheets and thirty changes of garments. If not, they would furnish Samson with the same.

The bride wept and teased, saying Samson did not love but hated her. He finally gave her the answer. She immediately told the men of the city. They taunted Samson until his anger kindled and he retaliated. Then he went up to his father's house.

Samson's mother grieved for him, even more when he went for his wife and found her father had given her to a companion Samson had thought was a friend. Was it for this he had been born? Nay. In spite of doubt, she remembered the angel's words and took comfort: he shall begin to deliver Israel out of the hand of the Philistines. Perhaps everything that had happened was according to a heavenly plan and a sign that deliverance had started.

DELILAH
JUDGES 16

Delilah of Sorek listened well when the lords of the Philistines came up unto her. Hatred filled their faces and spilled over into their words. "Entice the man Samson," they said. "See wherein his great strength lies, and by what means we may prevail against him. . . We will give thee every one of us eleven hundred pieces of silver."

Delilah's eyes glistened with greed. Such a paltry task! Was not Samson already entrapped by her charms? Knowledge of her power over men made the proposition even more attractive. Eyes half-closed, she envisioned the velvets and silks, gold chains, and rich jewels she would buy to enhance her perfumed body that drove men to madness.

When Samson came to her, Delilah began her campaign against the man who loved her. "Tell me," she began. "Where does it come from, the strength you possess? Should one wish to afflict you, how could it be done?"

Samson caressed her smooth cheek. "If I were bound with seven green withs that were never dried, I should be weak, and be as another man."

Delilah promptly reported the answer to the lords of the Philistines. They brought her the seven green withs that had not been dried. Men lay in wait inside her chamber and when Delilah bound Samson, she cried, "The Philistines be upon thee, Samson!"

He sprang to his feet, breaking the withs as if they had been single threads.

Delilah's face resembled a thundercloud. "Why do you mock me and lie to me? Tell me the truth, Samson."

This time he told her if his enemies bound him with new ropes that had never been used, he would be weak. She bound him, called out, and grew enraged when he broke them as easily as he had the withs.

Again she asked the secret of his strength, chagrined to find the power she thought she had over him had not yet been his undoing. Images of the vast fortune she had been promised faded.

Fury burned within her. It should not be so! She bound his locks, fastened them with a pin and watched Samson once more effortlessly free himself.

With tears and cajoling, Delilah vexed Samson until he told her all his heart. "There hath not come a razor upon my head; I have been a Nazarite unto God from my mother's womb: if I be shaven, then my strength will go from me, and I shall become weak, and be like any other man."

Delilah felt torn between hope and the fear it was only another lie but she reported to the Philistines, who brought the promised money. She made Samson sleep; a man came and shaved the luxuriant, uncut hair. This time when she cried, "The Philistines be upon thee," Samson awoke and said, "I will go out as at other times before, and shake myself." He did not know the Lord was departed from him. The Philistines took him away, leaving Delilah to gloat over her ill-gotten treasure.

No record is given of Delilah from that time forward. Historians can only speculate as to whether remorse filled her shallow, wicked soul when the Philistines put out Samson's eyes, bound him with fetters of brass, and brought him to Gaza. There he ground in the prison house, a beast of burden. His hair began to grow, as did his repentance.

Delilah may well have been one of the Philistine men and women who made sport of Samson and praised their gods for delivering him into their hands. If so, she died with Samson and the others when God heard Samson's prayer, "O Lord God, remember me. . .and strengthen me, I pray Thee only this once, O God, that I may be avenged of the Philistines for my two eyes." Taking hold of the middle pillars that held up the house, he bowed with all the restored might given by God. The walls crashed down, slaying the scheming lords and all with them.

NAOMI
RUTH 1-4

"Naomi, beloved." Elimelech turned a face filled with trouble toward his wife. "We cannot tarry in Bethlehem-judah any longer." Despair darkened his eyes. "Famine in our land continues, nay, grows stronger every day. We must take our sons and journey to the country of Moab. There we shall have—"

"Moab?" His good wife stared in disbelief. "Have you gone mad, my husband?" She glanced through the open doorway to where Mahlon and Chilion sat just out of hearing. "Where among the Moabites will our sons find proper wives?" Fear blanched her face and crept into her eyes. "Elimelech, this thing cannot be. Surely we must remain in our own country. Moab is filled with those who worship strange gods."

"There is food in Moab," her husband reminded. "To stay here is to starve." His gaze softened. "I like this journey no more than you, Naomi."

She said no more, but her mother's heart protested every mile of the way from Bethlehem-judah to the country of Moab, where they had to sojourn. Heavy of spirit, she prayed the famine would end so they might return home. Instead, they were forced to continue in a strange land, living among those who worshipped heathen gods.

During their stay, Elimelech died, leaving Naomi bereft and alone with her two sons. Her worst fears came to pass when Mahlon and Chilion took wives of the women of Moab. Although Ruth and Orpah were comely, they were of a different faith, which sorely grieved Naomi.

Ten years later, Mahlon and Chilion also died. Naomi rocked with grief. Why had Jehovah taken first her husband, then her sons? Now only the two daughters-in-law remained. What should she do? Word had come that the Lord had visited His people in the land of Judah and ended the famine. Her heart yearned within her. Oh, to return to her own country. Even the thought of it cheered her sad heart. Naomi made her choice. No longer would she dwell among those who worshipped false gods and bowed down to images of wood and stone.

The day of departure came. Although she had learned to love Orpah and Ruth, Naomi well knew the young women would surely wish to remarry. Better for them to remain in the land of Moab and find husbands among their own people. Naomi told them, "Go, return each to your mother's house: the Lord deal kindly with you, as ye have dealt with the dead, and with me. The Lord grant you that ye may find rest, each of you in the house of her husband." She kissed them.

Orpah and Ruth lifted up their voices and wept, saying, "Surely we will return with thee unto thy people."

Naomi shook her head. She told them they must stay. She had no husband, no more sons to offer as husbands for Orpah and Ruth. Even if she were to remarry and bear sons, there would be far too many years before they grew into manhood.

Tears fell, but Orpah at last accepted the parting. She kissed Naomi. Still weeping, she went back to her people and her gods. Ruth remained behind, cleaving unto the mother-in-law she loved more than life itself. Naomi could deny her no more. Together they started up the dusty road to Bethlehem.

RUTH
RUTH 1-4

"I have no sons to be your husbands," Naomi repeated to her tearful Moabite daughters-in-law.

Ruth scarcely heard her. Now that her husband lay in the grave, only Naomi remained to remind her of the happy years they had shared. She grew aware that Orpah had kissed the older woman and started back to her mother's house, as Naomi had told them to do. A wave of pain washed through her. She could not, would not, let her mother-in-law go without her.

Ruth fell to her knees before Naomi. She flung her arms around the other's legs and pleaded, "Intreat me not to leave thee, or to return from following after thee: for whither thou goest, I will go; and where thou lodgest, I will lodge: thy people shall be my people, and thy God my God.

"Where thou diest, there will I die, and there will I be buried: the Lord do so to me, and more also, if ought but death part thee and me."

In the silence that fell, Ruth held her breath, asking the God of her husband to soften her mother-in-law's heart. Gradually the stiffness of Naomi's body melted. With great joy, Ruth caught the words she had so longed to hear. "Arise, my child. We shall go to Bethlehem-judah together."

They spoke no more of Ruth's impassioned plea, and when they reached Bethlehem in the beginning of barley harvest, Naomi told those about them, "Call me not Naomi, but Mara, for the Almighty hath dealt very bitterly with me. I went out full, and the Lord hath brought me home again empty."

Ruth begged to go into the fields and glean ears of corn that they might have food. She came to land belonging to Boaz, a mighty man of wealth and a kinsman of Elimelech. Ruth heard words of praise for Boaz from many and counted herself fortunate to follow the reapers in his fields. She also secretly rejoiced when he sought her out.

"Daughter, go not to glean in another field. . .abide here by my maidens. I have charged the young men not to touch thee. Drink of the vessels which they have drawn when thou thirst."

Ruth fell to the ground. "Why have I found grace in thine eyes, that thou shouldst take knowledge of me, a stranger?"

Boaz told her he knew all she had done for her mother-in-law, that she had left her own father, mother, and land of nativity to come to a strange country. Ruth's heart stirred within her, the first time since the death of her husband. The comfort he offered showed she had found favor in his sight. She happily worked, not knowing Boaz had commanded his reapers to leave handfuls for her to glean.

Day after day Ruth gleaned in the fields, first barley, then wheat. Day after day she learned to admire Boaz more. When Naomi instructed her to wash and anoint herself and steal into the tent of Boaz while he lay sleeping, then uncover his feet and lie at them, she tremblingly obeyed. Boaz awakened to find her there. He told her to tarry the night and if the one who was a nearer kinsman than he would not take her to wife, then would he do this thing.

All night Ruth lay sleepless, hoping the other man would refuse her. To her great joy, that kinsman drew off his shoe and sold all that belonged to Elimelech, Mahlon, and Chilion to Boaz. Boaz proclaimed to the necessary witnesses that Ruth would be his wife.

On the day of the marriage feast, Ruth remembered her vow to Naomi and silently repeated it in her heart, only this time to her husband. She would truly make his lodge, his people, his God her own. Happiness filled her.

It increased when the Lord blessed Boaz and her with

a son. Naomi took the child, laid it in her bosom, and became nurse unto it. But Ruth praised the God of Israel she had come to know and called her son Obed, which means "worshipping God."

HANNAH
I SAMUEL 1-2

Hannah, wife of Elkanah, mourned. She knew she had her husband's best love. He had given her a worthy portion of the yearly sacrifice, far more than that bestowed on his second wife Peninnah, or to all her sons and daughters. If only she, wife of Elkanah's heart, could also give him children! Yet year after year when the family went up to the house of the Lord, Peninnah provoked Hannah until she wept and did not eat.

Elkanah said, "Hannah, why weepest thou? And why eatest thou not? And why is thy heart grieved? Am not I better to thee than ten sons?"

She took comfort, but sought out Eli, the priest, who sat by a post of the temple of the Lord. In bitterness of soul, she prayed and wept. She vowed that if the Lord of hosts would give her a man child, she would give him unto the Lord all the days of his life, and no razor would come upon his head.

Hannah spoke in her heart; only her lips moved. Eli thought her drunk. Hannah quickly denied it. "No, my lord. . .I have drunk neither wine nor strong drink, but have poured out my soul before the Lord."

Eli told her to go in peace. The God of Israel would

grant her petition. Hannah went her way. She ate, and sadness left her countenance.

Hannah conceived and bore a son. She called his name Samuel, saying, "Because I have asked him of the Lord." She did not go up to offer the yearly sacrifice and told Elkanah that when Samuel was weaned she would bring him before the Lord where the child would abide forever. At that time, Hannah took the child to Eli, the priest, repeating her vow and dedicating Samuel to God. She praised God, saying none was holy as the Lord and telling how her heart rejoiced.

Eli blessed Elkanah and Hannah, and the Lord visited her. She bore three more sons and two daughters. The child Samuel grew before the Lord, bringing greater rejoicing than ever to his mother's heart as he ministered unto the Lord before Eli the priest.

When Samuel was still a lad, the Lord called him three times. Samuel did not yet know the Lord, neither was the word of the Lord yet revealed to him. He ran to Eli, who told him after the second time that if the voice came again, he should say, "Speak, Lord, for Thy servant hearest." Samuel did as instructed and the Lord told him many things, including that Eli would be judged for the iniquity of his sons. Samuel hesitated to tell his friend, but Eli insisted.

Eli only replied, "It is the Lord: let Him do what seemeth Him good."

Samuel grew, and the Lord was with him. All Israel from Dan even to Beersheba knew Samuel was established to be a prophet of the Lord.

As gracious as the meaning of her name, Hannah continued faithful. Surely in her secret mother heart she missed and yearned for the son God gave her; the son she returned to a life of service in fulfillment of her vow. Hannah wisely overcame her longings with praise and a continual song before the Lord, telling of His power and goodness. Her song was handed down throughout the ages and remains a shining testimony of pure motherly love transcended only by the love of the Lord God of Israel, Almighty and Everlasting.

MICHAL
I SAMUEL 18-19; II SAMUEL 3,6

Michal, younger daughter of King Saul, loved David from the time she first saw him. Yet she knew she must lay her love aside. Her father had promised David the hand of Merab, his elder daughter. All of Michal's inner rebellion could not change things. She considered going to her father but hastily put aside the thought. Everyone knew of the rages that came upon Saul. Michal shuddered. She dared not chance having his wrath turned toward her.

Much had happened since the day David, son of Jesse, first stood before Saul. Ruddy, goodly to look upon, his beautiful countenance had attracted both Saul and young Michal. The king had sent to Jesse, saying, "Let David stand before me; for he hath found favor in my sight."

From that time on when the evil spirit entered Saul, David played softly on his harp. The music soothed and refreshed the king, and he became well. Saul loved

David greatly and made him his armor bearer.

Michal sighed. When had the corrosion of envy begun to enter Saul's heart, leaving it open to the evil spirit that vexed him? She sadly shook her head. Perhaps when the young shepherd had gone forth against the mighty Philistine, Goliath. A tender look of remembrance crossed Michal's face and a smile curved her lips. David had thrown aside the king's own armor, a helmet of brass and a coat of mail. Taking five smooth stones and his sling, he had slain the giant.

How her father had praised him—then. Michal thrilled at David's bravery, as she had scores of times before. She thought how her own brother Jonathan's very soul was knit with the soul of David. Her dark eyes glowed. Jonathan had stripped himself of garments, sword, and bow and given them to David as a token of the covenant of brotherhood between them.

Sadness replaced Michal's smile. Saul had set David over his soldiers, and all Israel and Judah loved David. A pang of fear went through her. She had seen her father's anger when the new young leader had returned from the slaughter of the Philistines. Women had come out of all the cities of Israel, singing and dancing, saying as they played on instruments, "Saul hath slain his thousands, and David his ten thousands."

The next day while in the throes of an evil spirit, Saul had thrown a javelin and barely missed killing the young man he had loved until mistrust changed everything. He had grown afraid of David, because the Lord was with him and had departed from Saul. The king had made him captain over a thousand and sent him from his presence. At that time, Saul had also promised Merab to David.

Michal felt hot shame when her father broke his vow and gave Merab to another, but she could not deny the spirit of joy that rose within her when Saul decided to give her to David instead. Nothing could make her happier.

Saul, the man God had called to reign over His people, had changed into a treacherous, bitter king. Jonathan stood between father and friend, true to his vow. Michal saved her husband's life by letting him down through a window when Saul's men came after him. She put the form of a man in her bed and said David lay sick when Saul sent messengers to take him.

Did Michal's heart break when her father gave her as wife to Phalti after David became an outlaw? And when David took first Abigail, then Ahinoam, as his wives? After Saul's death and David's anointing as king of Judah, he demanded Michal be returned to him. The Bible says her weeping husband went with her until he was sent back.

What memories filled the heart that had once been wholly David's? It appears love fled sometime over the years. Michal railed against David when she saw him dancing before the Lord. He responded by reminding her he was the king, chosen by the Lord. He vowed to be even more "vile." No wonder God had to give David a new heart before the shepherd who became king could change into the man God needed.

Michal had no children by David.

ABIGAIL
I SAMUEL 25, 27, 30

Few men were more blessed than Nabal. He owned three thousand sheep and a thousand goats. In addition, his wife Abigail not only had a beautiful countenance, but possessed good understanding. Nabal should have sung praises for all that was his as he sheared his sheep in Carmel. The churlish man did not and was known for his evil doings.

David, in the wilderness, mourning over Samuel's death, heard of Nabal. He called out ten young men and said, "Get you up to Carmel, and go to Nabal, and greet him in my name." He went on to tell them to extend peace to Nabal and his house and all he had and to remind Nabal how well David had treated the shepherds while they had been in Carmel.

David finished his instructions by telling the young men to say, "Give, I pray thee, whatsoever cometh to thine hand unto thy servants, and to thy son David."

Nabal listened to the words of David as given by the young men, then sneered. "Who is David? And who is the son of Jesse? There be many servants now a days that break away every man from his master. Shall I then take my bread, and my water, and my flesh that I have killed for my shearers, and give it unto men, whom I know not whence they be?"

This angered David greatly. He ordered 400 of his men to gird themselves with their swords and follow him.

One of the young men who served Nabal witnessed the exchange. He told Abigail how David had sent messengers out of the wilderness to salute the master but that Nabal had railed against them. He went on to tell her of David and his men's kindness and protection to Nabal's shepherds when they had been in the field. Nothing of Nabal's was missing during all the time they had tended the sheep. "They were a wall unto us both by night and day, all the while we were with them keeping the sheep," he earnestly reported. "Know and consider what thou wilt do; for evil is determined against our master, and against all of his household: for he is such a son of Belial* that a man cannot speak to him."

Anger at her husband's treatment of David's messengers surged through Abigail. She immediately took great quantities of food and loaded it on donkeys. She said nothing of her plan to Nabal but followed her servants. Heart beating in time with the hooves of the donkey she rode, she came down the hill and met David and his followers. Abigail dismounted and fell pleading at his feet to beg mercy. She told him she had been given no knowledge of the rude way his men had been treated and offered the food she had brought. She prophesied of the great things the Lord God of Israel would one day do with David.

David rejoiced that Abigail had kept him from shedding blood. He sent her to her house in peace. She found Nabal holding a great feast and drunken with wine. She told him nothing until the next day. His heart failed when he heard those things and ten days later he died.

Abigail later became David's wife. The mists of time obscure most of her life after that. We know she was one of many wives, bore a son called Chileab, was taken captive by the Amalekites, then rescued by David. Did she

*Belial: wicked, worthless

maintain the high courage that had first brought her to David's attention? The beautiful countenance? Or did years of having to share her husband with other women slowly grind her down? The story of how she lived up to the meaning of her name, "of strength," serves as an example of one unafraid to face the enemy and conquer by reasoning, rather than the use of weapons.

BATHSHEBA
II SAMUEL 11-12; I KINGS 2

"What shall I do?" The distraught woman hugged her arms across her breast and rocked to and fro. Fear smote her, tasting metallic in her mouth. "I shall be stoned, even though the king himself be responsible for my plight." The thought settled her whirling brain. Hope crept over into her troubled face. Surely David would not allow such a thing to happen! Making haste, she sent a message by a trusted servant. Four short words.

King David curiously opened the missive and read, "I am with child." He laid it aside, remembering. After the year of peace that had been declared, he had sent forth Joab, his servants, and all Israel into battle, but David had tarried at Jerusalem. One evening-tide, he had risen from his bed to walk on the roof of his house. He had looked down from his lofty domain and his blood had run hot, for a lovely woman had been washing herself. He had to discover who she was.

"Bathsheba, wife of Uriah the Hittite," had come the reply.

Her married status had not been able to quell the fire of David's desire. He had commanded that she be brought to him. Now she had conceived. What could he do? Even a king was not exempt from the punishment for adultery, which was death.

A scheme formed in his mind. He would bring Uriah back from fighting and send him to his wife, so that the evil David had done might not be discovered.

David's plan did not work. Uriah came, but slept at the door of the king's house with the servants. A conscientious soldier, he would not go to his home and wife while the ark of the covenant, his master Joab, and fellow companions camped in the open fields.

David hastily sent him back to Joab, carrying a letter that ordered the commander to put Uriah in the forefront of the hottest battle and leave him there to be smitten and die. Joab obeyed and it came to pass.

Bathsheba mourned for the husband she had lost, guilt-ridden, secretly glad he had never known that which had come upon her. When her mourning time ended, David took her as his wife. But the thing David had done displeased the Lord.

Fear again filled Bathsheba when Nathan posed a parable to the king that showed clearly he knew on whose order Uriah had died. Nathan made a terrible pronouncement: evil would rise against David out of his own house and all Israel would know.

The child Bathsheba bore unto David fell ill and on the seventh day died. Her mother's heart filled with anguish. This, then, was the price to be paid for sin. Not until David comforted her and she bore another son called Solomon did Bathsheba's sad heart find joy again.

Years later, when David was old, she fought for her son Solomon to be named king in place of Adonijah, who even then was taking over, for David was stricken in years and knew not what was happening. People were crying, "God save King Adonijah." King David swore by the Lord God of Israel that Solomon would sit on the throne in his stead. He ordered Solomon to be anointed as ruler over Israel and Judah.

Bathsheba bowed with her face to the earth. Triumph filled her soul. She did reverence to the king and said, "Let my lord King David live for ever."

After David's death, Solomon ascended to the throne. Adonijah sought Bathsheba out, saying he came in peace. He asked her to intercede with King Solomon that he might be given Abishag, David's Shunammite concubine, as his wife.

Bathsheba agreed. Solomon seated her at his right hand but grew enraged when she made the request. He told her she might as well have asked for the kingdom, then ordered that Adonijah be executed unless he bowed down to the rightful king, which he did. Nothing more is known of Bathsheba.

THE QUEEN OF SHEBA
I KINGS 10

Solomon's fame spread to the uttermost ends of the known earth. Tales of his wealth and wisdom ran far and wide. People spoke of his wisdom, that came about in this manner: In Gibeon the Lord appeared to

Solomon in a dream and said, "Ask what I shall give thee."

Solomon rehearsed the great mercy God had shown to his father David, according to when he had walked in truth, righteousness, and uprightness of heart. God had kept for David great kindness, even a son to sit on his throne.

"I am but a little child," Solomon confessed. "I know not how to go out or come in. Thy servant is in the midst of Thy people which Thou hast chosen, a great people, that cannot be numbered nor counted for multitude. Give therefore Thy servant an understanding heart to judge Thy people, that I may discern between good and bad: for who is able to judge this Thy so great a people?"

The request pleased God. He promised that since Solomon had not asked wealth or long life or the lives of his enemies, there would be none so wise as Solomon either before or after. God also blessed Solomon abundantly with the riches he had not sought, with honor, and length of days.

In faraway Arabia, the Queen of Sheba rested on soft cushions and narrowed her painted eyelids. Who was this Solomon, this man whose praise was sung by every passing caravan? She surveyed her surroundings. Did he, then, possess more than she? Was his palace more splendid, his robes of grander fabric and design? She laughed, mocking the thought. Did not the world know none was so mighty as the Queen of Sheba?

Yet a note of jealousy marred the laugh and with it a daring idea. Why should she not go to Jerusalem and see for herself? A single clap of the hands would bring a bevy of servants ready to do her bidding. Stay. She must consider well before embarking on the journey.

The Queen's curiosity waxed hotter with every wild tale. Even allowing for certain exaggeration, the kingdom of Solomon loomed ever more appealing in her mind. At last she ordered a great train to be prepared, camels bearing spices, and quantities of gold and precious stones. When she reached Jerusalem, she arrayed herself in her finest apparel and came to Solomon.

Armed with questions, the Queen shot them at the ruler whose fame had spread like fire in a field of ripe and waving wheat. Her observant eyes saw the splendor of his house, the food, all who served him, even the way by which he went up unto the house of the Lord. She hated to admit defeat, but what she saw forced her to do so. She said, "I believed not the words until I came. . . Behold, the half was not told me: thy wisdom and prosperity exceedeth the fame which I heard. Happy are thy men. . .thy servants which stand continually before thee, and that hear thy wisdom. Blessed be the Lord thy God, which delighted in thee, to set thee on the throne of Israel: because the Lord loved Israel for ever, therefore made He thee king, to do judgment and justice."

The Queen of Sheba gave Solomon great riches, but he gave her all that she desired, whatsoever she asked, beside that which Solomon gave her of his royal bounty. She and her servants turned and went to her own country.

Scripture records that the magnificence of Solomon's court impressed the Queen "until there was no more spirit in her." Perhaps this best shows the extent to which God blessed the king with material possessions. The magnitude of Solomon's wisdom, power and honor cannot be measured.

THE ZAREPHATH WIDOW
I KINGS 17

Only a poor widow, her name is unknown to those who handed down her story from generation to generation. Yet the widow who dwelt in Zarephath is revered by all who meet her in the first book of Kings. She gave all. Not because she could afford to give. The widow could not afford not to give.

God sent ravens to feed Elijah during the famine by which he was punishing Israel, telling him to hide by the brook Cherith, and drink from it. When the brook dried up for lack of rain in the land, God sent Elijah to Zarephath, saying, "I have commanded a widow woman there to sustain thee."

When Elijah reached the gate of the city, a widow woman bent low, gathering sticks. He called to her, "Fetch me, I pray thee, a little water in a vessel, that I may drink." She started to obey and he called again, "Bring me I pray thee, a morsel of bread in thine hand."

The widow stared at him. If only she could! Offering water was one thing; sharing food another. Her thin hands trembled, and she thought of the final bit of food in her possession. "As the Lord thy God liveth, I have not a cake, but an handful of meal in a barrel, and a little oil in a cruse. . .I am gathering two sticks that I may go in and dress it for me and my son, that we may eat it, and die."

"Fear not," Elijah told her. "Go and do as thou hast said: but make and bring me a little cake first, and after make for thee and for thy son. For thus saith the Lord God of Israel, 'The barrel of meal shall not waste, neither shall the cruse of oil fail, until the day that the Lord sendeth rain upon the earth.'"

The widow could scarcely believe her ears. Who was this stranger, to promise such a thing? Was it a deception to gain the last of her food? She looked into his face. Something caused her to do his bidding. She slowly took out the meal and oil to make a cake for the stranger, but there yet remained other meal and oil. She marveled, prepared food for herself and her child and thanked the God of Israel. For many days, each time the household hungered, the widow closed her eyes in fear, then rejoiced and baked cakes from the never-empty barrel and cruse.

Her blessings did not end with food. After these things, the widow's son fell ill until his breath left him. She called out in pain, asking why Elijah had done so unto her. He took the child to a loft and laid him upon the bed. He then cried to the Lord, stretched himself upon the child three times and said, "O Lord my God, I pray thee, let this child's soul come into him again."

Elijah took the child, and brought him down out of the chamber into the house, and delivered him unto his mother. Then Elijah said, "See, thy son liveth."

The widow raised her head, bowed with weeping. She stilled her mourning and received her child with great joy. Her heart overflowed with gratefulness and she said unto Elijah, "Now by this I know that thou art a man of God, and that the word of the Lord in thy mouth is truth."

And it all began with a handful of meal and a little oil in a cruse.

JEZEBEL
I KINGS 16, 18-19, 21; II KINGS 9

Ahab, son of Omri, reigned over Israel twenty and two years. It is written he "did evil in the sight of the Lord above all that were before him," surpassing the wickedness of anyone up to that time. Marrying Jezebel and embracing her gods ranked first on his list of sins.

The name Jezebel has been known throughout history as a synonym for dark deeds and treachery. It is not hard to picture a scene such as this.

Jezebel, silken, perfumed, jeweled, lolling on richly embroidered cushions. Painted face. Long fingernails stained as red as if dipped in blood. Physically beautiful enough to tempt any man not dedicated to a God higher than those she served. A hundred plots milling in her scheming, clever brain. A dozen maidens clustered around her, freakish imitations of Jezebel's sensuous charm.

"I will marry Ahab himself," she predicts. Her eyes glitter with assurance of her power over men. "I shall be queen of all Israel. What better way to establish the true religion, the worship of Baal?"

A murmur ripples through the bevy of maidens, but no one dares disagree. Jezebel's streak of cruelty and supreme vanity permits no criticism. She reigns her private kingdom by fear, not through admiration of those who serve and fawn upon her.

"Ahab shall build a house of Baal in Samaria and set up an altar to him." Jezebel whips herself into a frenzy. Hot color pours into her cheeks and a gleam that spells disaster for anyone who gets in her way comes to her eyes. "Ahab shall also make a grove. . ." She allows her voice to trail off and a self-satisfied smirk tilts her red, red lips.

The maidens clap their hands. Their eyes glisten. Only too well do they know the dancing, cavorting, and unholy actions in the groves dedicated to the heathen gods the Israelites despise. "Will such a thing not provoke the God of Ahab?" one, more daring than the rest, asks.

Affronted, Jezebel sternly reminds them, "There is no god like Baal." She sinks her white teeth into her painted lower lip and plans more evil.

How she rejoices when Ahab does as she asks! How she boasts. She cuts off the prophets of the Lord, all except the hundred Obadiah spirited away, hid in a cave, and fed bread and water. She laughs at famine and drought, little caring that many suffer because of her and Ahab. She hates Elijah with all the fury of one who knows her own vileness but will not tolerate anyone speaking of it. If fear crosses her mind when he challenges her gods, she hides it, and exultantly anticipates the confrontation on Mount Carmel between her 450 prophets of Baal and 400 of the grove. This day will Baal defeat the Israelite God forever!

It does not happen. All morning, the prophets cry for Baal to send fire and consume the offering on the altar. Nothing happens, even though they scream until hoarse and leap on the altar.

At noon Elijah mocks the false prophets, taunting that their gods must be asleep or talking or perhaps away on a journey. The priests slash their bodies and Jezebel shrieks at them to conquer. That evening Elijah builds an altar in the name of the Lord. Three times it is soaked with water. After a simple prayer, fire comes from heaven and consumes everything, including the water in the trench. The people fall on their faces, crying, "The Lord, He is the God." Elijah slays every false prophet and the rain returns.

Jezebel's fury knows no bounds when Ahab tells her what has happened. She threatens Elijah's life and laughs when he prophesies her violent end. Years later, vain to the last, she paints her face and taunts Jehu, the new king, from her window. Perhaps she feels her aging charms will save her. Is there regret in her heart when the eunuchs who sympathize with Jehu lift her up and throw her from the window? If so, is it for her wickedness or only her loss of power and life? No one knows. . .and as Elijah prophesied, the dogs wait below.

THE SHUNAMMITE WOMAN
II KINGS 4

"Sir, I beg of you to eat bread with us," a woman of Shunem pleaded with Elisha when he came to her village.

Elisha turned aside and ate with the woman, who was highly respected by all who knew her. She immediately beseeched the prophet to honor her home by eating with them whenever he came to Shunem. And so Elisha ate at the woman's table.

The good woman perceived he was a holy man of God, who passed by continually. She told her husband,

"Let us make a little chamber, I pray thee, on the wall; and let us set for him there a bed, and a table, and a stool, and a candlestick: and it shall be, when he cometh to us, that he shall turn in thither."

The next time Elisha came, he entered the chamber and lay there. After a time he ordered his servant Gehazi, "Call this Shunammite." When she stood before him, Elisha spoke of how carefully she had provided for him. He asked, "What is to be done for thee? Wouldst thou be spoken for to the king, or to the captain of the host?"

"I dwell among my own people," she answered.

Again Elisha asked, "What then is to be done for her?"

Gehazi, who had remained silent during the interchange, spoke. "Verily she hath no child, and her husband is old."

For the second time Elisha called her. When the woman stood in the door he said, "About this season, according to the time of life, thou shalt embrace a son."

The woman stared at him, then shook her head. "Nay, my lord," she sadly replied. "Thou man of God, do not lie unto thine handmaid."

Great was her joy when even as Elisha had predicted, she conceived a bore a son in due season.

One day when the child grew older, he went out to his father who was with the reapers. Suddenly he clutched his head and groaned.

"My head, my head!"Alarmed, his father ordered a lad to carry him to his mother. The stricken son sat on her knees till noon, then died. The good woman refused to accept his death. She laid him on Elisha's bed, shut the door and went out. "Send me one of the young men," she ordered her grieving husband. "And one of the asses, that I may run to the man of God, and come again."

The husband couldn't understand. He asked why she would go on that day. But the great woman only said, "It shall be well." Commanding the young man driving the donkeys not to hesitate for her, she went and came unto Mount Carmel.

Gehazi, the servant, met her when she was yet afar off from the man of God. He told her Elisha had seen her and told him to inquire if all was well. She valiantly replied all was well, but caught Elisha by the feet when she came to him, in spite of Gehazi's protests. She refused to leave him until Elisha rose and followed her. Gehazi passed on before them and laid his master's staff on the child's face but came back wearing a long face. The child had not awakened. By the time Elisha came into the house, the child lay dead.

The Shunammite woman waited while Elisha went in and lay upon the child, with his mouth on the child's mouth, his eyes on his eyes, and his hands on his hands. The child's flesh grew warm. Elisha repeated the process. From without the chamber, the woman heard a sneeze. Another, and another, seven in all. Her heart leaped within her breast. Surely her child lived! Elisha called her in. She beheld her son, then fell at the prophet's feet and bowed to the ground. The son granted by God's mercy had been spared.

THE ISRAELITE MAID
II KINGS 5

"Why do you weep, my mistress?" a little captive maid of Israel, handmaiden in the house of Naaman, captain of the host of the king of Syria, timidly asked. Although she often longed for her own people, she had learned to love Naaman and his wife. He was a great man with the king and honorable. By him the Lord had given deliverance unto Syria. He was also a mighty man in valor and kind to those who served him.

Now the little maid's mistress lay sobbing as if her heart would break. Again the girl asked, "Why do you weep?"

"Leprosy has come upon Naaman," his wife stammered.

Leprosy! Dreaded and feared by all. And yet—the little maid's heart beat high. She spoke quickly. "Would God my lord were with the prophet that is in Samaria, for he would recover him of his leprosy."

The suffering woman raised dazed eyes to her maid, a feeble hope springing to her face. They scarcely noticed that one who overheard hastily left the chamber. The man repeated word for word what the little maid had said.

Naaman could scarcely believe it, yet anything was better than watching the awful sickness creep over him. He told the king of all Syria, who immediately sent him with a letter to the king of Israel, asking that he heal Naaman.

The Israelite king rent his clothes. He was no God;

neither had he the power to cure leprosy.

Mistress and maid waited, hoped, and prayed. Day after day passed. Their hearts sang when Naaman returned unto them. Not a trace of the terrible disease remained. The little maid stood near her mistress while he told his story.

"The king could do nothing, but a man named Elisha said for me to come to him. I came with my horses and chariot and stood by the door of his house." A rueful look went over his face. "Elisha didn't even come outside. He sent a messenger telling me to go wash in the Jordan seven times and my flesh would come again to me and I would be clean."

The little maid's eyes rounded. Her mistress gasped. "How strange! Did he not know who you were?" she disbelievingly asked.

"He had given his command," her husband told her. "I was wroth, but still thought he would come forth, call on the name of the Lord his God and strike the leprosy from my body. If I must wash in a river, why the Jordan? Are not the rivers of Damascus better? When he did not come, I went away in a rage."

"But you are healed!" his wife protested.

Naaman's voice softened. Wonder came into his eyes. "Ah, my brave servants came near and said, 'My father, if the prophet had bid thee do some great thing, wouldest thou not have done it? How much rather then, when he saith to thee, Wash and be clean'?"

"I hearkened unto them. I dipped myself in the Jordan. Once, twice, until I rose from the water six times. The leprosy remained." His face took on a look of awe. "The seventh time I rose straightway out of the water clean and purified! This time when I went to the prophet's house, he came out. I said to him, 'There is no God in all the earth, but in Israel.'"

The little Israelite maid clapped her hands in joy. Many times she wondered, was it for this she had been taken into captivity? To be the instrument by which Naaman would find Elisha and be healed? The thought comforted her, and she continued to serve those who never tired of expressing appreciation that she had told them about the prophet of the true and living God.

HADASSAH
ESTHER 1-10

Hadassah, also known as Esther, "the star," had neither father nor mother but dwelt in the house of her cousin Mordecai, who treated her as a daughter. The were of the captive nation of Judah and living in Persia. One day Mordecai said, "The king has sent a decree throughout the land. All wives are to give honor to their husbands. Queen Vashti refused to come at the king's command when his heart was merry with much wine. She has been banished."

Esther felt a tiny pulse beat in her throat.

"All the fair young virgins are to be gathered unto Shushan the palace, to the house of the women. The maiden which pleaseth the king shall be queen instead of Vashti. Esther, think what it would mean should you be chosen."

A flush went over the beautiful face. As queen, she

could help her people.

"Do not tell the king you are Jewish," Mordecai warned.

After twelve months of purification rites, Esther went to the king. She so found favor with him that Ahasuerus loved Esther above all the women. He set the royal crown on her head and made her queen instead of Vashti.

Mordecai, who often stood outside the palace gate to hear news of his cousin, learned that two of the king's chamberlains who kept the door planned to lay hands on Ahasuerus. He told Esther, who informed the king. The culprits were hanged and the deed written in the king's chronicles.

Haman, a courtier set above all the princes of the kingdom, hated Mordecai. The Jew would not bow to him. Haman told lies to the king about the Jews and convinced him that the Jewish men, women, and children should be destroyed on a certain day.

Mordecai donned sackcloth and ashes. When Esther sent to know why, he told her of the king's command. He warned that even she could not escape. She sent back and asked all Jews to fast for her. On the third day, she went and stood in the court. She prayed God would grant that the king would extend his scepter to her. If he did not, she could die for daring to approach him. The king summoned her forward.

Esther invited both him and Haman to a banquet. Once they were there, she made a petition, inviting them to a second banquet the next day. That night the king, unable to sleep, read his chronicles and discovered the service Mordecai had done for him. He also realized Mordecai had never received a reward. The next day, he asked Haman what honor a loyal man should receive. Haman named great things, thinking it would all be for him—then had to see it all bestowed on Mordecai.

At the second banquet that night, Esther courageously exposed Haman's plot. She confessed that she also was Jewish and subject to the decree.

The king immediately hanged Haman on a gallows Haman had constructed for Mordecai and gave Mordecai Haman's house and his own royal ring. Yet he had no power to reverse the order he had given concerning the slaughter of the Jews, for it had been written and sealed with the king's ring. All he could do was grant the Jews in every part of the land permission to defend themselves.

This he did. He also sent Mordecai out from his presence arrayed in royal apparel and with a great crown of gold. The Jews rejoiced.

No enemy could withstand the fierce fighting of the Jews, once given a decree to defend themselves. Fair and lovely Esther's bravery saved not only her life, but the lives of her people. Her story stands today as an example of one who fearlessly believed God and did all she could to right the wrongs done her people, even when her actions could have led to her own death.

AN ISRAELITE MOTHER
DANIEL 1-3, 6

Many times far more can be learned about a woman's life from the actions of her children than what is recorded concerning her personally. Such is the case of four Israelite women, especially Daniel's mother. The light of her calling to motherhood shines steady and bright through the life of her son.

Nebuchadnezzar, King of Babylon, sat on his throne and pondered. Suppose he tried an experiment. His clever mind turned a growing idea over and over, then he called his chief court official to him. "Bring me children of Israel who are of royalty. They must have no blemish, but be well favored, wise, and cunning. They must understand science and have ability to stand in the king's palace and learn our language." A curious smile brightened his face. "We shall see what comes to pass."

All that he commanded was done. Young men, carefully selected, were transplanted from their native land to Babylon. For three years they would have a daily portion of the king's meat, and of the wine he drank. So nourished, they would then stand before the king.

Among the Israelites were Daniel and three who became Shadrach, Meshach, and Abednego. How did their mothers feel, seeing the sons they had borne and nursed taken away to a land of heathen customs? Surely many prayers went with the young men.

Picture a parting scene between Daniel and his mother: "My son, forget not all thy father and mother have taught thee. Forsake not Jehovah, the One true God."

Daniel bows his head. "I shall forget neither thee nor thy teachings."

"Peace be unto you," the mother brokenly tells him.

"And to you." He walks away, then turns, raises one hand in farewell, and disappears from the home he loves. From henceforth, his dwelling shall be among strangers.

A niggling worry attacks the watching mother. She cries out in a voice so low only God can hear. "Lord God of Israel, hear my plea. Has this, thy servant, prepared her son to face what lies ahead?" She shivers, imagining a hundred unknown dangers. "I cannot go with him, Lord. I cannot cradle his tired head against my bosom or soothe him in times of perplexity. Only thou, O God, canst make him strong." She strains tear-dimmed eyes, but her son is gone.

The courts of Babylon are like nothing the young Israelite men know. Daniel clings to the fact he has found favor with the chief official, who has been set over him, Shadrach, Meshach, and Abednego. He sees sympathy in the man's eyes. That and their mothers' teachings give him and his companions the courage to stand the first of many hard tests.

"Why do you refuse the king's meat and not drink of his wine?" the anxious official demands. "The king will have my head should you look worse than the other young men."

They explain such eating and drinking would defile them. From childhood, they have eaten pulse (vegetables) and drunk water. Daniel proposes that for a time they be given only pulse and water. At the end of ten days, they will compare their health with that of the others. The official agrees. To his amazement, all four stand strong, and straight, and none of the others are like unto them.

Test after test comes. Yet always the knowledge of praying mothers and the early teachings so important to the young Israelites' development into manhood serve them well. By the power of God revealed in a night vision, Daniel interprets a dream King Nebuchadnezzar cannot even remember how to tell. Daniel and his faithful friends refuse to worship the king. God closes lions' mouths and later sends One to walk with the children of Israel in the fiery furnace so not one hair on their heads is singed. The kingdom marvels. In uprightness of heart, those men—brought up in the fear of the Lord by godly mothers—despise heathen gods and ways. They cling to their early teachings and glorify Jehovah in word and deed.

THE IDEAL WOMAN
PROVERBS 31

In a male-dominated world where only the most outstanding (or notorious!) women received much attention, Solomon offers a glowing portrait of the ideal woman. His tribute also elevates everyday tasks and describes the value of those who strive to live up to their God-given womanhood.

Although written to those who lived long ago, much of Proverbs 31:10-31 remains applicable today. The New International Version of the Bible aptly titles this section of scripture "The Wife of Noble Character."

> A wife of noble character who can find?
> She is worth far more than rubies.
> Her husband has full confidence in her
> and lacks nothing of value.
> She brings him good, not harm,
> all the days of her life.

She selects wool and flax
  and works with eager hands.
She is like the merchant ships,
  bringing her food from afar.
She gets up while it is still dark;
  she provides food for her family
  and portions for her servant girls.
She considers a field and buys it;
  out of her earnings she plants a
  vineyard.
She sets about her work vigorously;
  her arms are strong for her tasks.
She sees that her trading is profitable,
  and her lamp does not go out at night.
In her hand she holds the distaff
  and grasps the spindle with her fingers.
She opens her arms to the poor
  and extends her hands to the needy.
When it snows, she has no fear for her household;
  for all of them are clothed in scarlet.
She makes coverings for her bed;
  she is clothed in fine linen and purple.
Her husband is respected at the city gate, where
  he takes his seat among the elders of the land.
She makes linen garments and sells them,
  and supplies the merchants with sashes.
She is clothed with strength and dignity;
  she can laugh at the days to come.
She speaks with wisdom,
  and faithful instruction is on her tongue.
She watches over the affairs of her household
  and does not eat the bread of idleness.

Her children arise and call her blessed;
    her husband also, and he praises her:
"Many women do noble things,
    but you surpass them all."
Charm is deceptive, and beauty is fleeting;
    but a woman who fears the LORD
    is to be praised.
Give her the reward she has earned,
    and let her works bring her praise at the
    city gate.

MARY, THE MOTHER OF JESUS
MATTHEW 1; LUKE 1-2

Clip-clopping hooves of a little donkey chosen more for strength than beauty sent spirals up from the dusty road on which two travelers plodded. Mary shifted in a vain attempt to find a more comfortable position. "I pray we shall reach Bethlehem soon," she told the sturdy man who walked beside her.

"It is not far now," he encouraged. A slight frown wrinkled his sweaty forehead. "Is it well with thee and thy babe?" He anxiously glanced at her cumbersome body, great with child.

"It is well." She smiled at her husband and smothered a small, secret sigh. The journey from Nazareth had been long and hard. Swarms of people crowded the roads and made traveling difficult. Rich and poor, healthy and sick, old and young, all sought their birthplace to be counted and taxed, for the decree of Caesar Augustus exempted no one.

The little donkey plodded on, one ear drooping. Mary rested against the rolled blankets Joseph had thoughtfully strapped on the donkey and the strong hand he placed against her back. Weariness swept over her like waves on the Sea of Galilee, blurring the present, recalling the past. . .

Mary slowly opened her eyes. Had someone called? Nay. Quiet lay over the room like a shimmering veil. And yet—

"Hail, thou that art highly favored, the Lord is with thee: blessed art thou among women." A glowing figure stood beside her.

Mary shrank in terror. What manner of salutation might this be?

The angel—for such he must be—said, "Fear not, Mary: for thou hast found favor with God. And, behold, thou shalt conceive in thy womb, and bring forth a son, and shalt call his name JESUS. He shall be great, and shall be called the Son of the Highest: and the Lord God shall give unto him the throne of his father David: And he shall reign over the house of Jacob for ever; and of his kingdom there shall be no end."

She, bear a child? Although she was espoused to Joseph the carpenter, they had not yet become man and wife. "How shall this be, seeing I know not a man?" Mary asked, unable to tear her gaze from the shining figure.

The angel replied, "The Holy Ghost shall come upon thee, and the power of the Highest shall overshadow thee: therefore also that holy thing which shall be born of thee shall be called the Son of God."

He went on to tell her, "Behold, thy cousin Elisabeth, she hath also conceived a son in her old age: and this is the sixth month with her, who was called barren. For with God nothing shall be impossible." Truth radiated in every word.

Belief and acceptance stirred in Mary's heart. The Lord God of Israel Who had created the earth and the heavens, Who had parted the sea and fed His children in the wilderness, possessed power that knew no bounds. "Behold the handmaid of the Lord; be it unto me according to thy word," Mary whispered. Joy and trembling filled her soul and she bowed in humility. When she raised her head, the angel had departed from her.

After a time of pondering all the things the angel had said, Mary knew what she must do. "I will arise and go to Elisabeth," she decided. So began a time of newness for the Jewish maiden. Her visit with Elisabeth confirmed the truth of all she had been told, yet a great wall rose in Mary's life. Could Joseph, loving and kind as he was, believe what had come upon her? Or would he think her a bad woman, one who sought to cover her sins with wild tales?

In fear and trembling, Mary related all the angel had said. She saw the shock in Joseph's eyes, the pain and disappointment that one he had thought pure should come to this sad state. Should he make her a public example, she would be stoned. What, then, would become of the babe she carried, the child the angel had said was the Son of God?

A just man who loved Mary with all his heart, Joseph considered the matter day and night. He was minded to put her away privily for he could not bear to see her stoned, even if she had sinned against heaven and against him.

While he thought on these things, the angel of the Lord appeared unto him in a dream. "Joseph. . .fear not to take unto thee Mary thy wife: for that which is conceived in her is of the Holy Ghost."

The angel spoke other things, confirming Mary's story, then departed. Joseph raised from his sleep. He wanted to climb to the rooftops and shout to any who might listen, "She is innocent! My Mary is pure and chosen among all women to bear a son who shall be called Emmanuel, 'God with us.'" When he told Mary all that had come to pass, they rejoiced together.

In the months that followed, Mary found herself in a strange state. She hugged knowledge to her heart and marveled. Sometimes her heart beat until she thought it might burst. Why had she, of all the virgins in Nazareth, nay, in the entire land, been chosen to bear the Son of God? She thought of other maidens, older and more experienced than she, worthy and devoted. Would she be able to succor and care for the child in the proper way? Yet each time doubts came, the razor-sharp memory of the angel's visit, the words that had burned into her heart, rose to reassure her. And each time, she bowed herself and humbly prayed she might be worthy of the great honor and responsibility to which she had been called...

"Mary." A gentle hand pressed her shoulder. She returned from her remembrances. "We have reached Bethlehem."

A sharp pain tore through her. "It is a good thing," she gasped and laced her fingers together over her swollen belly.

"Hasten, little friend," Joseph told the donkey who obligingly broke into a faster pace. Yet as the three travelers went from inn to inn and found no place, Mary fought ever-increasing pain. At last a kindly innkeeper offered them a place in a dry, warm cave where he kept his animals. By then Mary little cared for anything except a place to rest and deliver her child. What mattered it whether he be born in inn or stable? She must have shelter and soon.

Before the cock crowed, Mary brought forth her first-born son. She wrapped him in swaddling clothes, and spent, she held him close, sensing the present moment might be the most precious of her life. A little later, she roused to voices. Shepherds knelt before her, faces working, eyes turned toward the babe. They told her angels had proclaimed the baby's birth while they had been in the fields keeping their sheep. They glorified God and praised Him. Mary tucked their visit away in her heart to be pondered later.

From glory to agony, from childbearing through Jesus' childhood to the cross and beyond, Mary, mother of Jesus, is history's finest reminder that with God nothing shall be impossible.

ELISABETH
LUKE 1

Mary's cousin Elisabeth lived with her husband Zacharias in the hill country of Judah. Word of their righteousness spread throughout the land for they walked blameless in all the commandments and ordinances of the Lord. Yet one thing they lacked: a child. Elisabeth was barren and both she and Zacharias were aged.

Zacharias served in the priest's office and burned

incense in the temple of the Lord. One day an angel appeared and stood on the right side of the altar. Fear fell on the old priest. But the angel said, "Fear not. . .thy prayer is heard: and thy wife Elisabeth shall bear thee a son, and thou shalt call his name John."

The angel said John would be great in the Lord's sight, many would rejoice at his birth, and he would be filled with the Holy Ghost even from his mother's womb. But Zacharias could not believe. "Whereby shall I know this, for I am an old man, and my wife well stricken in years?"

The angel announced that he was Gabriel, sent by God. Because of Zacharias' unbelief, he would be dumb—unable to speak—until all had been accomplished.

Elisabeth conceived. Great was the old couple's joy, but the priest remained dumb. Elisabeth sang at her work and dreamed of the day she would deliver her firstborn. How good God was to remove her barren state and thereby take away her reproach!

In the sixth month, Mary came to pay Elisabeth a visit. The moment Mary saluted her cousin, Elisabeth felt her babe leap within her. She blessed Mary and the babe she carried within her. Mary responded with a song of praise.

For three happy months, Mary dwelt with Elisabeth. How they talked, the two who had been chosen to be mothers in Israel: one of the Son of God, the other of one who would turn many hearts toward the Lord. After Mary returned to her home, Elisabeth brought forth a son. Her heart swelled when her neighbors and her cousins heard how the Lord had showed great mercy. They rejoiced with her—but Zacharias remained dumb.

Would he ever speak again? Elisabeth wondered. She contented herself in caring for her son, little heeding those who protested when she said he should be called John.

"There is none of thy kindred called by this name," they protested, when on the eighth day the child was brought for circumcision.

They appealed to Zacharias. He signed for writing materials and confirmed the baby should be called John. Immediately his tongue loosed. He praised God and prophesied of that to come.

Elisabeth cherished her son, yet she never forgot the prophecies concerning him. Scripture does not tell whether she lived to see John grow and wax strong in spirit. Did she watch him enter the desert in which he would abide until his time came? Was she one who entered the waters of baptism at his hand? If alive at the time, surely she agonized when an act of wanton wickedness ended his ministry. All that is known is the exemplary life of this godly mother of John the Baptizer who fulfilled her role and rejoiced at having been blessed in her old age.

ANNA
LUKE 2

For fourscore and four years, Anna the prophetess departed not from the temple, but served God night and day. Once she had been married, but after only seven years, her husband had died. Each year of service saw her grow a little older and a little slower. Yet she refused to let the ravages of time force her to leave off her fasting and prayers. What dreams did she dream? What knowledge did she gain during her years in the temple and well over 80 years of living? The things she saw in that long time span would surely fill many volumes.

One day Mary and Joseph brought their little son to the temple. Anna watched Simeon, who had been told he would not see death before he had seen the Lord's Christ, take Jesus in his arms and bless Him.

Anna's heartbeat quickened. She crowded closer. "Thanks unto the Lord," she cried. Strength beyond her years filled her. She spoke of the child called Jesus to all who looked for redemption in Israel. Simeon's words echoed in her ears, "Lord, now lettest thy servant depart in peace, for mine eyes have seen thy salvation which thou hast prepared before the face of all people; a light to lighten the Gentiles, and the glory of thy people Israel." Perhaps Anna's heart echoed Simeon's cry. Once she had seen Jesus' face, what more had life to offer?

A WOMAN OF FAITH
MATTHEW 9; MARK 5; LUKE 8

She knelt before Jesus in fear and trembling, an insignificant woman in the midst of a multitude. Desperation and fear had driven her to seek the new prophet, whose wonders were being whispered, shouted, and sung throughout her land. At first she had scoffed. Was not Jesus the son of a Nazarene carpenter?

"Yea," those who spoke to her confirmed, "yet He is

WOMEN OF THE BIBLE

much more."

She considered well whether to present herself to this man of whom she knew nothing except gossip. Would it not be better to go on without hope than to allow herself to believe the Teacher might have a cure for the rare blood disease that had plagued her for twelve endless years?

Physician after physician had examined her, sadly shaken their heads, and said they could do nothing. Each time, she had died a little more inside. Why such a thing had come upon her, she knew not. Apathy often caused her to ask, "Does it matter? Soon I must die and that will be the end."

Memories of a time before the illness had destroyed her dreams danced before her. Oh, to once again run free and well through the fields. To walk without weakness, to straighten to full height and to move without pain. *It cannot happen if you do not keep seeking a cure*, a voice whispered in her heart.

One evening when she lay sleepless, the woman decided, "I will arise in the morning and seek this Jesus. I will cast myself at His feet. If He is all people say, He will have mercy on me. If not, I will die and the pain will be no more." She knew it would require her last measure of strength to travel even the short distance to Jesus.

In spite of her determination, and in spite of her belief that Jesus was her last and only hope, the stricken woman's heart quailed at the sight of the throng surrounding the One she sought. She felt weakness wash through her as waves that wash against the shore during a storm. She could go no farther.

A slight opening in the crowd gave her a glimpse of

WOMEN OF THE BIBLE

Jesus. It was enough to renew her. *If I may but touch His garment, I shall be whole,* she said in her heart. She stretched forth her hand. The edge of Jesus' cloak felt rough against her searching fingers. Strength flowed into her. She opened her mouth to cry out she had been healed, but no words came.

Jesus, immediately knowing that virtue had gone out of Him, turned and said, "Who touched my clothes?"

His disciples replied, "Thou seest the multitude thronging Thee, and sayest Thou, who touched Me?"

But Jesus looked round about to see her that had done this thing.

She knelt before him in fear and trembling. "Lord, it was I. I knew if I could but touch the hem of your garment, I would be healed." Head bowed, she waited. What would He do?

Jesus spoke in a voice like unto none she had ever before heard. "Daughter, be of good comfort; thy faith hath made thee whole."

Her faith? Words hung on her quivering lips, the confession of how little faith she had possessed. She looked into Jesus' face, filled with compassion and understanding that swept away any need for explanations.

Tears rained like skies weeping for an unbelieving world. She again bowed her face to the ground, only vaguely aware when the multitude moved on—some following Jesus to ask for blessing; others out of curiosity. Then she stood, praised God and ran, rejoicing with each breath of air that filled her lungs and every long stride that carried her on her way.

JAIRUS' DAUGHTER
MATTHEW 9; MARK 5; LUKE 8

J airus loved his daughter with a love known only to those who have been blessed with one child. When she was stricken with illness, he nearly went mad with grief. She must not die, this child whose twelve short years had blessed his household mightily.

"I will seek out Jesus of Nazareth," he said. "If all the tales of Him are true, He will surely heal my child."

When he reached Jesus, the crowd made way. Was not Jairus one of the rulers of the synagogue? Jairus fell at Jesus' feet, worshipped, and besought him greatly, saying, "My little daughter lieth at the point of death: I pray thee, come and lay Thy hands on her, that she may be healed; and she shall live."

Jesus arose and followed Jairus, as did His disciples.

On the way, a disturbance came in the crowd. Jairus seethed with impatience. To one in his daughter's condition, every moment mattered. Why must a tottering woman slow them? The next moment he caught his breath. The woman who had barely grazed the hem of Jesus' garment with her fingertips was made whole! Jairus' heart leaped within him. If the Master could heal with only that slight touch, how much more would He do when He laid hands on the child who lay just outside the gates of death?

Jairus' heart sang, then turned to stone when some of his own household rushed out saying, "Thy daughter is dead: why troublest thou the Master any further?" An unworthy thought crept into his mind and took lodging. Why had Jesus tarried to heal the woman and allowed a child to die? Was the woman's life of more importance than the maiden's?

Did Jesus perceive his thoughts? Perhaps, for He spoke. "Fear not: believe only, and she shall be made whole."

Jairus stumbled on, torn between the assurance in Jesus' eyes and the utter impossibility of the dead being restored to life. When they at last reached Jairus' home, Jesus permitted only Peter, James, John, Jairus, and his wife to come into the chamber. All the rest wept and wailed, and when Jesus said, "Weep not; she is not dead, but sleepeth," they laughed Him to scorn.

Jesus ordered them all out. He took the maiden by the hand, and called, saying, "Maid, arise."

Her spirit came again, and she arose straightway: and Jesus commanded her parents to give her food.

Jairus felt faint with astonishment and joy. He saw from his wife's face that she felt the same. When they attempted to thank Jesus, He charged them they should tell no man what was done. But the fame of Jesus' raising Jairus' daughter went abroad into all that land.

HERODIAS
MATTHEW 14; MARK 6

Many were those Herodias, ex-wife of Philip, now married to Philip's brother, hated. Her legendary rages effectively quelled opposition for fear of the retribution she mercilessly dealt out to any who dared speak against her. Yet of all her foes, none loomed larger in her twisted mind than John, the Baptizer.

Each time Herodias thought of the wild prophet who had come from the wilderness to thunder and stir up the people, she gnashed her teeth in fury. "How dare he speak against us?" she demanded of Herod, her brother-in-law and husband. "If you do not care that he cries in the streets that you are breaking the law, what about me? Should not the tetrarch have the right to take whatever woman he desires, whether or not she be married to his brother?" She clenched her hands with their painted nails until they became claws, working as if she had her enemy's throat between them and would throttle out John's life.

"Be still," Herod commanded. "You know how powerful John has grown. The multitude who believe in him and count him a prophet daily grows larger." He hesitated and spread his hands in a helpless gesture. "Is it not enough that I had him bound and thrown into prison?"

"Pah! It will never be enough," she retorted. "He has insulted and attempted to shame us before all the people. He must pay with his life. You should have had him executed long since."

"I tell you, I cannot," Herod roared.

Herodias only sneered, secretly despising him for his weakness. If she'd had the power to order John's death, she would have done so the moment he had dared raise his voice and condemn those he should bow to and worship. "Are you then afraid of him?"

"Nay," Herod lied. "But the Baptizer is a just man and holy." He did not add that he had observed John, even heard him gladly, until the prophet had publicly denounced him for his adultery.

Herodias said no more at the time. Yet with each passing day, she hated John more and vowed to do him harm in whatever way she could.

Plot after plot came to mind. She would know no peace until John's body lay in the ground and his impudent tongue was forever silenced. Even from his cell, he continued to cry out against her and Herod for their illicit relationship.

Herodias brazenly kept the silken curtains of her litter open when she was carried through the city streets. She stared into the faces of those she passed, and her wrath against John increased. For although Herod's subjects bowed low in obeisance, their scornful expressions and the epithets hurled at her from the security of the multitude brought flags of scarlet to her vapid, painted face.

"I will bide my time," she vowed. "Then I will strike." Again she curled her sharp-nailed fingers into claws and anticipation spread over her like honey warmed in the sun.

SALOME
MATTHEW 14; MARK 6

Salome clasped her hands in delight. "I am really to dance before the court?"

Herodias smiled a curious smile. "Yes, my pet. You must dance as you have never danced before. Much is at stake."

Salome failed to catch any particular significance in

her mother's voice. To dance before Herod was great enough honor. To be chosen to perform at the great feast the tetrarch had ordered in honor of his birthday overwhelmed her. Some of her confidence fled. "What if I do not please him?"

Herodias eyed her daughter's beauty, her slim and graceful figure. A gleam came to her calculating gaze. "You shall please him." She tossed her head and laughed. "Herod and the lords, high captains and chief estates of Galilee, will be so drunken with wine a damsel with far less charms than you could entertain them. You must do much more, Salome. You are to dance in a way not seen in the court, one that entices and drives men mad at the sight of you. Do you hear?"

A deep flush rose in the girl's smooth cheeks. An uncanny resemblance to the mother who demanded adulation as her due showed in her countenance. "I hear and obey." She half-closed her eyes, already planning how she could be more daring, more seductive than all those who had preceded her in Herod's court.

On the great day, Herodias carefully ordered her daughter to remain secluded until time for her dance. She watched and waited, a jeweled spider decked out in royal raiment. Wine flowed like the Jordan in spring. Now came the moment for which Herodias waited. She dared not prolong Salome's entrance much longer or Herod would be too drunk to fully appreciate the young girl's ravishing dance.

"Now," she beckoned.

Salome burst upon the court in the most sensuous dance ever performed. She saw men's eyes widen with lust for her barely concealed body. She saw Herod's hot gaze fasten itself on her and she danced on, until he called her to him. "Ask of me whatsoever thou wilt, and I will give it thee." He held his cup for more wine and swore, "Whatsoever thou shalt ask of me, I will give it to thee, unto the half of my kingdom!"

Salome's eyes glistened. Half the kingdom, for her? She opened her mouth to speak, to request jewels, riches beyond belief. Nay, first she must consult with her mother. Much wiser in the ways of the world, Herodias would advise her daughter well.

"What shall I ask?" she demanded of Herodias.

"The head of John the Baptizer."

Salome recoiled. Her eyes widened. Her breath came in labored gasps.

"Do as I tell you," Herodias commanded. "For your sake as well as mine. Should the people take it into their heads to stone me, you will not be spared. The Baptizer must be silenced if we are to live." Triumph gleamed in her eyes.

Terrified at the threat, Salome straightway hurried back to the king. "I will that thou give me here in a charger the head of John the Baptizer."

Silence fell over the court. The shock in Herod's eyes showed that Salome's demand had partially sobered him. Regret clouded his face and he opened his mouth, glanced around the gathered guests, and halted. Salome followed his thoughts. He might be willing to give the other half of his kingdom to undo his rash promise, but he would not. To do so would make him an object of contempt.

Herod gave the command. Soon after, the executioner returned. For a moment Salome stared at the platter. She drove her teeth into her lip to keep down nausea. She closed her ears against the horrid sounds of retching by those sober enough to care. In silence so heavy it hung like a shroud, Salome turned, fixed her gaze straight ahead and carried her gruesome burden to an ecstatic Herodias.

No one knows if Salome ever wept bitter tears or was haunted by nightmares for her evil deed. History only records that she danced and John paid with his life for daring to speak out against evil wherever he found it, even in the highest places.

THE CANAANITE WOMAN
MATTHEW 15; MARK 7

For many years a woman of Canaan cared for her daughter. Grievously vexed with a devil, the girl writhed and threw herself back and forth, wailing and gnashing her teeth until her mother thought she would die. Sometimes her secret heart wished she would. Death could surely be no worse than life as the maiden lived it.

Why had they been so cursed? All who dwelt on the coasts of Tyre and Sidon knew their story and shunned them. How long must a mother watch the one she had given life being destroyed by a devil?

"There is a Jew called Jesus who travels in the land," a neighbor told the distraught woman after the worst spell her daughter had ever suffered. She lowered her voice, as if afraid to be overheard. "It is said He heals those who come to Him."

The mother laughed bitterly. "A Jew heal the daughter of a woman of Canaan? Such a thing could not be!"

Yet as the attacks increased, she knew she must pursue every rumor on behalf of her daughter.

When the woman came to Jesus, she immediately began to cry in a loud voice, "Have mercy on me, O Lord, thou son of David; my daughter is grievously vexed with a devil," then she held her breath waiting for His reply.

Jesus answered not.

She cried again.

The disciples, impatient with her pleadings, besought Jesus, "Send her away; for she crieth after us."

But He answered and said, "I am not sent but unto the lost sheep of the house of Israel."

The woman's hope flickered like a lamp with only a few drops of oil. Should she leave off beseeching Him? Nay. Better to risk the wrath of the One she implored than go away heavy-hearted. She fell at Jesus' feet and worshipped Him, saying, "Lord, help me."

Jesus answered and said, "It is not meet to take the children's bread and to cast it to dogs."

Goaded by her great need, the woman refused to be silent. She refused to let Jesus walk away, for if He did, all hope would go with Him. "Truth, Lord: yet the dogs eat of the crumbs which fall from their master's table."

She dared not look up, dared not risk looking at Jesus or the disciples who indignantly murmured against her that she should speak so to the Master.

Then Jesus answered and said unto her, "O woman, great is thy faith; be it unto thee even as thou wilt." And her daughter was made whole from that very hour.

The woman of Canaan is a permanent reminder of how love and concern for others and faith born of despair can prevail even when circumstances appear hopeless.

THE TEN VIRGINS
MATTHEW 25

The ten virgins—five wise, and five foolish—are characters in a parable Jesus told. A parable is "an earthly story with a heavenly meaning."

"Good friends, our lamps are growing dim," a maiden said to her companions. "We must go forth, buy oil, and fill them lest they go out before the bridegroom cometh." She reached for shawl and veil.

Four of the nine virgins she addressed straightway rose up. They went with her into the marketplace and purchased oil to replenish their supply.

"Why do you make haste?" the other five wanted to know. "It is yet day. The bridegroom tarries. There is plenty of time to fill our lamps before he comes." They chattered and laughed together, poking fun at the five virgins industriously filling and polishing their lamps until they shone brightly.

The hour grew late and the household became weary, but no word came from the expected guest. At last, all retired and fell into deep slumber.

At the midnight hour, a great cry sounded throughout the streets of the city. "Behold, the bridegroom cometh; go ye out to meet him."

The ten virgins immediately arose and joyously trimmed their lamps. The five who had failed to fill their lamps cried, "Give us of your oil; for our lamps are gone out."

The others shook their heads. "Not so; lest there be not enough for us and you: but go ye rather to them that sell, and buy for yourselves."

The five foolish virgins who had whiled away their time in mocking their wiser sisters wasted no more time. They rushed into the marketplace, pounded on an oil merchant's door, and clamored for him to open his shop that they might purchase oil.

The door remained shuttered; the shop dark and bare.

"We must have oil," the frightened girls told one another. "We will try another merchant."

While they were out attempting to buy oil, the bridegroom came. Great was the joy of the five virgins who were ready and waiting for him. They went in with him to the marriage and the door was shut behind them.

From dark street to dark street the foolish five ran, beating on doors, trying to rouse anyone who might sell or lend them oil for their empty lamps. They railed against their five wise sisters, saying they should have shared their oil. Yet they knew in their hearts if the situation were reversed, they would not dare give away precious oil and risk not having enough for themselves.

What little oil had remained in their lamps had long since vanished. Heavy of heart, the five virgins turned toward home, hoping for some miracle to fill their lamps that they might be found ready to be admitted to the marriage feast.

At last they reached the house. The door stood firmly shut. All their trying could not open it. "Lord, Lord," they implored, "open to us."

But He answered and said, "Verily I say unto you, I know you not."

Five foolish virgins huddled together in outer darkness, weeping bitterly at having lost their chance simply because they had not prepared during the time given to make ready.

Historians say a faithfully observed custom in those days was the setting of the marriage time by the bridegroom. He chose any day within a two-week period and made ready, then sent a messenger to announce his arrival. All ten virgins surely knew the custom. Five prepared ahead of time. The other five acted on the premise that there was no hurry, with dire results—offering a lesson well worth heeding.

PILATE'S WIFE
MATTHEW 27

First, restlessness. Then, dreams without form or substance, more terrifying than any the wife of Pontius Pilate, the governor of Judea, had ever known. "No. No!" A scream burst from her throat and tore the fabric of sleep to shreds. She bolted upright and threw back the silken bed coverings that threatened to smother her.

"Mistress, what is it?" Maidens in her service ran to the chamber, eyes enormous in their white faces.

Slowly the hard beating of her heart stilled enough for her to whisper, "Where is my husband?" Perception sharpened by the dream that yet clutched at her with frightening fingers, she caught their hesitation and quick exchange of glances.

"Answer me," she ordered, with an imperious gesture.

"Even at this moment he questions a prisoner," one faltered.

"The man called Jesus?"

"Yea."

She sank back against her cushions and waved them away, feeling the blood drain from her face. Jesus, who haunted her dreams until she felt she would go mad. The distraught woman pressed her hands to her aching temples. Why had Pontius Pilate ever consented to accept the post of procurator here in this miserable land? Her lip curled. Enemies in high places were surely responsible for the ignominious assignment. Ever since they'd arrived, there had been nothing but trouble. In his ignorance of those he had been sent to rule, Pilate had made one mistake after another and incurred the hatred and wrath of his subjects.

"I cannot think of it," the tormented woman cried. Yet how could she not think of it? The entire land of Judea rang with gossip concerning the man who now stood in the judgment hall before her husband.

"Just another rabble-rousing Jew," Pontius had said when told the chief priests and elders took counsel against Jesus to put Him to death. Yet in spite of his bold statement, he had shifted uneasily. "I don't like this. They bring their squabbles to me when they should be solving them. What good are they if they cannot settle their own disputes?"

"It is more than that," his wife had pointed out. "This Jesus has spoken out against the Pharisees and scribes, calling them corrupt, whited sepulchers."

"Perhaps He should be praised rather than condemned." Pilate had smiled sardonically. "That bunch of hypocrites is no more qualified to lead than the swine they despise." He'd sighed. "What must be will be. They have no authority to give an execution order."

"So they come to you," she'd bitterly told him.

"Yea." He'd stridden out, leaving her to ponder.

Now the wife of Pilate slid from her couch and clapped her hands. When her maidens came running, she ordered them to bring her writing materials and hastily wrote: "Have thou nothing to do with that just man: for I have suffered many things this day in a dream because of Him."

"See this is taken to the governor at once," she commanded, then paced the floor of her luxurious rooms a long, weary time until slow, heavy steps announced the coming of her husband. Before he entered, she could tell things had not gone well.

"I washed my hands of it," he mumbled. "I told the multitude I was innocent of the blood of the just man. They said, 'His blood be on us, and on our children.'" He stared at his shaking hands, called for a pitcher and water, and washed his hands again.

She said nothing. Pontius continued in a voice so dead it brought shivers to her body. Misery shone in his dull eyes. "I found no fault in Him, but what could I do? They said I was no friend of Caesar if I released Jesus. It is over."

Nay, his wife's heart shouted. *Your misery—and mine—is only beginning.*

WOMEN OF THE BIBLE

MARY MAGDALENE
MATTHEW 27; MARK 15-16; JOHN 20

Mary Magdalene, out of whom Jesus had cast seven devils, writhed with pain. The Master had done so much for her. Why could she not do more for Him? Although she, along with a few other women, had followed Jesus and ministered to Him, all they could do now was stand helplessly by and watch him die on the cross between two thieves.

She and Mary the mother of Joses had sat near the sepulcher, silently grieving. Now, at home, the Sabbath passed slowly. How could life continue? Mary thought of herself before Jesus had healed her, of the spells that had come over her without warning and turned her into a mad woman. All it had taken to free her was a single touch. She could still feel the warmth that had flowed through her, healing her spiritually and cleansing her of all sin.

At last the Sabbath had passed. On the first day of the week, at the rising of the sun, Mary Magdalene joined Mary the mother of James and a friend named Salome. Carrying sweet spices to anoint Jesus' body, they came near to the sepulcher. "Who shall roll away the stone from the door of the sepulcher that we may enter?" one asked. The women looked at one another in dismay. After Jesus had died and was taken from the cross, Joseph of Arimathaea, an honorable counselor who also waited for the kingdom of God, had boldly gone to Pilate and asked for the body of Jesus. The governor had agreed. Joseph had brought fine linen, and had taken Jesus down, and had wrapped Him. He had laid Jesus in a sepulcher hewn out of rock. A great stone had been rolled unto the door, and guards had been set by Pilate. Three women, no matter how determined, would not be able to move the stone.

"Behold!" Mary pointed, gasping for breath. "The stone has been rolled away!"

"How—when—where are the guards?"

The entrance to the sepulcher looked wide and empty. The women looked at each other and hesitantly stepped inside. They fell to their knees in fright, for a young man clothed in a long, white garment sat on the right side. His countenance was like lightning, and his raiment white as snow.

"Be not affrighted," he said. "Why seek ye the living among the dead? He is not here, but is risen: remember how He spake unto you when He was yet in Galilee, saying, 'The Son of man must be delivered into the hands of sinful men, and be crucified, and the third day rise again.' But go your way, tell His disciples and Peter that He goeth before you into Galilee: there shall ye see Him, as He said unto you."

Marveling, unable to believe what they had seen and heard, the women fled. Mary Magdalene went straight to Simon Peter and John. "They have taken away the Lord out of the sepulcher, and we know not where they have laid him," she cried. In broken phrases, she told the disciples what the angel had said. Peter and John hastened to the sepulcher, but only the linen clothes and napkin lay as mute evidence One had been there. Unable to understand it, they went to their homes.

Mary could not bear to leave. She stood without the sepulcher weeping, then bent down and looked in. Two angels in white sat, one at the foot, the other at the head of where Jesus' body had lain. They asked why she wept and she repeated, "Because they have taken away my Lord, and I know not where they have laid him." Blinded by her tears, she turned and faced a man she supposed to be the gardener.

He said, "Woman, why weepest thou? Whom seekest thou?"

She pleaded for him to tell her where Jesus had been taken, but He said unto her, "Mary."

That voice! Joy flooded her soul. "Rabboni!" ("Master!")

"Touch Me not, for I am not yet ascended to My Father," Jesus said.

Heart pounding, she ran and found the disciples. They believed not, for they had not seen. But Mary of Magdala knew Jesus lived again, even as she lived anew when Jesus cast out the seven devils and made her a new creature in Him.

A DESPERATE MOTHER
JOHN 9

Each time her son went forth to beg, his mother's heart ached. Was it not enough that God had cursed him with blindness from birth? Why must he also be forced to beg? She sighed. There was no other choice. She and her husband between them could not earn enough to provide even the rudest shelter, the coarsest food without the pittance the son brought in.

"Better to die and be out of this miserable life," she

muttered.

Strange tales came to their household, of a teacher said to heal. Neighbors told stories passed on from those who claimed to have stood by and seen Jesus of Nazareth touch the infirm and make them whole. Something stirred within the blind man's mother. She hastily pressed it down. Even Jehovah did not heal those blind from birth. Yet her gnarled hands stilled at her work and she caught herself dreaming. Suppose. . .

"Nay," she chastised herself. "Such a thing cannot be, although I am desperate enough to try anything. Perhaps I should seek out this teacher and see for myself if He does the miracles they say."

One day she went to the place where her son sat begging. A little crowd had gathered in front of the spot her son occupied. The mother heard someone ask, "Master, who did sin, this man, or his parents, that he was born blind?"

Anguish went through the listening mother. Had she not asked herself the same question as many times as there were stars in the sky? She numbly waited for the answer that would confirm and condemn her.

A rich voice replied, one filled with compassion and authority. "Neither hath this man sinned, nor his parents: but that the works of God should be made manifest in him. . ."

The woman elbowed her way through a resentful crowd until she stood near her son. She watched the Man whose back was to her stoop spit on the ground, and make clay of the spittle and dirt. She gasped when He anointed the eyes of her blind son and commanded, "Go, wash in the pool of Siloam."

Paralyzed by shock, the mother saw her son struggle to his feet. She watched him make his way to the pool. He splashed water on his face, removing the last bits of clay clinging to his eyes. The next instant a shriek rose to the heavens. "I see!" He leaped in his gladness. "Praise God, I can see!" He ran toward home on feet made fleet by joy.

When his mother arrived, panting from her exertion, her son stood in a circle of neighbors babbling questions, wondering if this were really he who had been blind. The seeing man told what had happened, yet some could not believe this, their neighbor, had received sight. "Where is the One who healed you?" they asked, but the son knew not.

"My son!" His sobbing mother clasped him in her arms, feeling her bitterness vanish when their tears mingled. It gave her strength to face the Pharisees when they came claiming Jesus was a sinner and not of God. Had he not healed on the Sabbath? They did not believe the man had ever been blind. "Is this your son, who ye say was blind? How then doth he now see?"

The glad mother and father stood their ground, although trembling with fear. These religious leaders had agreed that anyone who confessed Jesus was Christ should be put out of the synagogue. They told the questioners their son had indeed been born blind. They could not explain why he now saw. "He is of age; ask him: he shall speak for himself," they told the Pharisees.

Their son reminded them God does not hear sinners; if Jesus were not of God, He could do nothing. The Pharisees cast him out, still mumbling against Jesus, but the little family rejoiced at the healing of their son.

Jesus later came to the man he had healed. The son believed and worshipped Him. Did the desperate mother and her husband also accept Him as the Son of God? Perhaps, for Jesus healed far more than their son as He passed by.

THE POOR WIDOW
MARK 12; LUKE 12

J esus loved to watch people. He yearned over them and longed for them to break the bondage formed by sin and be free. He rejoiced when they listened to Him and laid aside their burdens, prejudices, and hypocrisy. He wept when they turned away—but always, He watched.

One day He sat watching those who came to the treasury and cast in their money. He noticed the careless way the rich flung in much, then went away with heads held high, proud to have done their duty so magnificently. Perhaps He sadly smiled, knowing they had their reward by being seen and noted for their generosity.

A poor widow hung back until the more worthy finished making their offerings, then she timidly came forward. Evidences of poverty showed in her clothing; the workworn hands obviously knew great toil. Her tired fingers fumbled in her cloak and drew forth two mites, which make a farthing.

For a moment, she stared at the small amount of money, then cast it in with the rest. She disappeared into the crowd, little dreaming her deed would be known until time ran out.

Jesus called unto Him His disciples. He said to them, "Verily I say unto you, that this poor widow hath cast more in than all they which have cast into the treasury."

The disciples looked at one another in amazement. How could the two mites, which make a farthing, compare with the golden coins thrown into the treasury by those of great wealth?

Jesus went on to explain. "All they did cast in of their abundance; but she of her want did cast in all that she had, even all her living."

As the widow of Zarephath had given the last of her meal and oil to the prophet Elijah, so the woman in Jesus' time had given everything she had. If she could speak to us down the path from the past, perhaps this devoted servant would tell of blessings as great as those experienced by her giving counterpart who lived hundreds of years earlier.

A WOMAN OF THE CITY
LUKE 7

A woman of the city known to be a sinner learned Jesus of Nazareth had consented to eat with Simon, a Pharisee. She considered and planned what she would do. The Master deserved tribute; she had the means to give it to Him.

While they sat at meat, she entered Simon's house, carrying in both hands her most precious possession: an alabaster box of ointment. She stood at Jesus' feet and wept, then washed His feet with her tears. She used her long and lustrous hair to dry them, then kissed the Master's feet and anointed them with ointment.

Simon glared at her. She could read his displeasure in the gaze he turned toward her. To have such as she dare enter his home and minister to Jesus was beyond decency. If He were the prophet people proclaimed, surely He would know her for a sinner and refuse to allow her to touch Him.

Jesus suddenly spoke, addressing his host. "There was a certain creditor which had two debtors: the one owed five hundred pence, and the other fifty. And when they had nothing to pay, he frankly forgave them both. Tell me therefore, which of them will love him most?"

Simon answered, "I suppose that he to whom he forgave most."

Jesus smiled. "Thou hast rightly judged." He turned to the woman, but said unto Simon, "Seest thou this woman? I entered into thine house, thou gavest me no water for my feet: but she hath washed my feet with tears, and wiped them with the hairs of her head.

"Thou gavest me no kiss: but this woman since the time I came in hath not ceased to kiss my feet. My head with oil thou didst not anoint: but this woman hath anointed my feet with ointment.

"Wherefore I say unto thee; her sins which are many, are forgiven; for she loved much: but to whom little is forgiven, the same loveth little."

Jesus said unto her, "Thy sins are forgiven."

The woman kneeling at his feet could speak no word. Never since she'd become notorious had a man spoken to her so. She felt as though she had stepped under a fall of clear water, cleansing and pure.

A quick glance around the circle of watching guests showed their confusion, their inner wonderings of who Jesus could be to forgive sins.

Jesus told her, "Thy faith hath saved thee; go in peace."

Somehow she managed to rise and sedately leave the room, although she longed to leap into the air and cry out with joy. Somehow she made her way down a street that looked far different than when she had trod it on the way to Simon's abode. Jesus' admonition rang in her ears. "Go in peace." *Peace!* Something she had dreamed about and never thought to find. Now, in a twinkling, it had come.

The alabaster box was empty, but the woman's heart was filled to bursting. A new life beckoned. She raised her face to the sky and ran to greet her vastly changed future.

MARY OF BETHANY
LUKE 10; JOHN 11-12

Mary and her sister Martha's reputation for hospitality was known throughout their village. They delighted in opening their home to passers-by in need of food and lodging. The women invited Jesus to stay with them any time He came to Bethany.

Mary delighted in sitting at Jesus' feet and hearing His word—even when Martha needed help with preparing and serving food and the many tasks necessary to keep a household in good order.

Martha loved to have Jesus stay with them, but it meant much extra work. At times she felt overwhelmed by the magnitude of the task she faced. Sometimes Jesus' disciples accompanied Him. Always curious neighbors dropped by. She could not send them home at meal times for fear of her being considered ill-mannered, so she had to feed them too.

On one such occasion, Martha's resentment rose to a full boil. More than the usual number of guests had appeared, and where was Mary when most needed? Where else? Sitting at the Master's feet, listening to His words.

A pang went through Martha and a lump formed in her throat. If only she could also sit at the Master's feet and hear what He said. Why didn't Mary realize the burden she placed on her sister? Why didn't she offer to take her place supervising the endless chores, the roasting and baking, breadmaking and serving? A little voice inside reminded her she wasn't being fair. Mary did do her share of cooking and cleaning. She just couldn't bear to be out of Jesus' sight when He came, even to help with the serving.

"Suppose I just walked away from my tasks and joined her?" Martha muttered. "Fine thing. None would be given food or drink until their bellies loudly protested."

Cumbered about with much serving, Martha came to Jesus. "Lord, dost Thou not care that my sister hath left me to serve alone? Bid her therefore that she help me."

Mary rose, a stricken look on her face. It was always thus. She became so engrossed in the Master's words as He spoke with her brother Lazarus and others who gathered, she forgot her duties. Like a child, she stood with bowed head and quivering lips. What must Jesus think of her? She scarcely dared raise her head enough to look at either Him or Martha.

Jesus hesitated a long moment. He sighed and spoke in a voice that held more sadness than condemnation. "Martha, Martha," He said. "Thou art careful and troubled about many things—"

Mary saw the pleased look creep over her sister's face. Such was high praise from the Master. But why did He address Martha, instead of her slothful sister?

Mary held her breath and Jesus continued.

"One thing is needful: and Mary hath chosen that good part, which shall not be taken away from her."

The constricting bands about Mary's heart loosened at His words. She caught quick tears in Martha's eyes, the look of shame at having complained. Martha looked cut to the quick.

Tender-hearted Mary sprang to her sister's side. She wrapped her arms around Martha. "I will help you," she promised. "Then we both shall sit at Jesus' feet."

Readers of the Mary and Martha story often dwell on Jesus' rebuke to Martha and praise of Mary. Yet Jesus did not consider Martha a bad person. On the other hand, He freely praised her for being "careful and troubled about many things." When He pointed out one thing was needed in her life, it didn't mean for her to give up doing the daily chores that required attention. Jesus well knew the necessity of hard labor from lessons learned at Joseph's knee in the carpenter shop and from watching His mother perform household duties.

In saying Mary had chosen that good part that would

not be taken from her, Jesus wanted Martha to focus on what was even more important. He would not always abide in the home at Bethany. Martha must learn to store up His teachings, as Mary did, against the time of His departure. Everyday duties would always abound. The opportunity for the sisters to hear Him would not.

MARTHA
LUKE 10; JOHN 11-12

Lazarus lay ill, little caring about or responding to his sisters' tender ministrations. In spite of everything they had done, he grew worse. Martha and Mary called a servant and ordered, "Go to Jesus and say unto Him, 'Lord, behold, he whom thou lovest is sick.'" They watched the servant hasten to obey, a measure of comfort stealing into their hearts. In a short time, Jesus would come and all would be well.

Minutes dragged into anxious hours, but Jesus did not come. "Did you not make clear how sick Lazarus is?" Martha demanded of the servant.

"Yea, mistress."

"Then why does He not come?" she cried. "It has been two days."

Lower and lower Lazarus sank until no life remained in him. Martha and Mary could not understand why Jesus tarried along the way. They sadly prepared their brother for burial, hot tears falling on the linen wrappings. They laid him to rest in a cave and rolled a stone before it. The entire household went into mourning for the brother and master who would be with them no more.

"Jesus could have saved Lazarus," Martha bitterly told Mary.

"I know." Her sister sighed, eyes filled with trouble.

Many of the Jews came to comfort the bereaved women. Days later, word came that Jesus was nigh unto Bethany. Martha laid aside her tasks and hurried to meet Him, but Mary sat still in the house. When Martha reached Jesus she burst into tears. "Lord, if Thou hadst been here, my brother had not died. But I know, that even now, whatsoever Thou wilt ask of God, God will give it thee."

Jesus said unto her, "Thy brother shall rise again."

"I know." Martha sobbed, desolate at the loss of the brother she had loved and cared for for so long. "He shall rise again in the resurrection at the last day."

"I am the resurrection, and the life; he that believeth in me, though he were dead, yet shall he live: and whosoever liveth and believeth in me shall never die. Believest thou this?"

All Jesus' teachings rushed back to confirm the truth to the sorrowful woman. She cried in a voice that held not only faith but knowledge. "Yea, Lord: I believe that thou art the Christ, the Son of God, which should come into the world." Then she went back to the house and whispered to Mary, "The Master is come, and calleth for thee."

Jesus had not yet entered the town. When the Jews saw Mary rise up and go to meet Him, they murmured, "She goeth unto the grave to weep," and followed her, as did Martha.

Mary reached Jesus and fell at His feet. "Lord, if Thou hadst been here, my brother had not died."

Jesus groaned in the spirit, and was troubled. "Where have ye laid him?"

The Jews said, "Lord, come and see."

Jesus wept, and the Jews murmured among themselves, "Behold, how He loved him!" But some said, "Could not this man, which opened the eyes of the blind, have caused that even this man should not have died?"

Martha's broken heart echoed the question over and over as she stumbled after Jesus on the way to the grave.

"Take ye away the stone," Jesus commanded.

"Lord, by this time he stinketh: for he hath been dead four days," Martha protested.

Jesus told her, "Said I not unto thee, that, if thou wouldst believe, thou shouldest see the glory of God?" Martha didn't understand and shrank back when the stone, with much grinding, moved away from the grave.

Jesus prayed to His Father in heaven, then cried in a loud voice, "Lazarus, come forth." Martha gasped and huddled close to Mary. The watching Jews stood as if frozen. A white figure appeared, bound hand and foot with graveclothes and face covered with a napkin. "Loose him and let him go," Jesus ordered. In fear and trembling, it was done. Lazarus stood before them, strong, whole, resurrected from the dead.

With one accord, those present fell to the ground. They rubbed their eyes, unable to believe what they saw. Many of the Jews who had come to comfort Mary and Martha, but had seen the things Jesus had done, believed on Him from that day.

It is interesting to note that Martha, once gently reproved by the Master, showed such strong faith that she cried affirmation from the midst of tragedy. Out of a broken heart came her unshakable belief in the resurrection.

Too often Martha is remembered as a woman so busy with household duties she didn't take time to listen to Jesus. She should be remembered for her valiant testimony that Jesus was the Son of God.

THE WOMAN AT THE WELL
JOHN 4

The Samaritan woman turned slow steps toward Jacob's well. She hated going there. Her neighbors pulled their skirts aside when she passed by, and they murmured against her. Yet she must have water if she was to live, and the sixth hour was as good a time to draw water as any.

Raising her head, she noted a man sitting nearby. He looked tired. His garments showed him to be a Jew. Dread filled her. It was bad enough being the object of scorn among her own kind, but the smug, self-righteous Jews who came to the well as they passed through Samaria made her feel less than the dirt beneath their sandals. She silently stepped forward to draw water so she could leave at once. A pleasant voice halted her, saying, "Give me to drink."

She looked full in His face and her lips curled. "How is it that Thou, being a Jew, askest drink of me, which am a woman of Samaria? For the Jews have no dealings with the Samaritans." *If the stranger had the brains of a donkey he would know this and not have to be told.*

"If thou knewest the gift of God, and Who it is that saith to thee, 'Give Me to drink,' thou wouldest have asked of Him, and He would have given thee living water," He told her.

Living water? Amazed at His manner of speaking she retorted, "Sir, Thou hast nothing to draw with, and the well is deep: from whence then hast Thou that living water? Art Thou greater than our father Jacob, which gave us the well, and drank thereof himself, and his children, and his cattle?"

Jesus told her whoever drank water from Jacob's well would thirst again, but those who drank of the water He would give should never thirst. He said, "The water that I give him shall be in him a well of water springing up into everlasting life."

Why should the strange words churn her spirit? Suppose this magician could give her water so she never again had to thirst, or to come to the well and draw? She impulsively pleaded with Him to do so, but Jesus bade her to go, call her husband and come back to the well.

Shame reddened her face, and she cast her gaze downward to escape His piercing look. "I have no husband." To her amazement, He responded she had spoken well, for although she had had five husbands, the man she now had was not her husband.

Fear came upon her. "Sir, I perceive that Thou art a prophet."

He expounded many things to her. With each truth, her spirit kindled until it flamed into response. "I know that Messiah cometh, which is called Christ: when He is come, He will tell us all things."

Jesus said, "I that speak unto thee am He."

WOMEN OF THE BIBLE

The woman straightway left her waterpot. She raced to the city and said unto the men, "Come, see a man which told me all things that ever I did: is not this the Christ?" She ran to others, proclaiming what had come to pass that day to all who would listen. They went out of the city and came unto Him. Many believed on Him by reason of the woman's testimony. They besought Him to tarry and Jesus abode there two days.

Many more believed because of Jesus' own word, for they had heard Him themselves, and knew He was indeed the Christ, the Savior of the world. The Samaritan woman found a niche in history because she listened to, believed, and shouted the truth of Jesus, the Christ, through the streets of her city.

THE WOMAN ACCUSED
JOHN 8

The wretched woman brought to the temple by the scribes and Pharisees dared not raise her head, yet in spite of her terror, she felt a certain sense of release. Today would end her miserable life. If it weren't for the agony to come with the sharp stones hurled by men no better than she, she wouldn't care. Perhaps the gods would be merciful and allow the first to stun or fell her with a blow to the head.

"Master, this woman was taken in adultery, in the very act. Now Moses in the law commanded us that such should be stoned: but what sayest Thou?"

A long stillness followed, so lengthy the accused woman risked a quick glance at the Teacher someone in

WOMEN OF THE BIBLE

the crowd had addressed as Jesus. He looked kinder than those who had taken her, but it would avail nothing. A law was a law, not to be broken. She thought bitterly of the man with whom she had been found. Why was he not here as well? Had those who had taken her conveniently allowed him to escape?

The silence continued, then a slight rustling sound came from Jesus' robe as He stooped down and, with His finger, wrote on the ground, as though He heard them not.

The captive wondered, but the scribes and Pharisees continued railing against her, demanding that Jesus answer.

He raised up, and said unto them, "He that is without sin among you, let him first cast a stone at her." He stooped down again and wrote upon the ground.

The woman's mouth fell open. Little as she knew about Jewish law, she realized Jesus had challenged those who had brought her to be judged with the sharpest challenge imaginable. Not that it would benefit her. Some of these self-righteous men considered themselves so holy they wouldn't recognize sin in their hearts if it stung like the desert scorpions.

She tensed, waiting for the first missile to tear into her flesh. Someone coughed. Feet shuffled. She felt movement and raised her head. Jesus still stooped down, busy with writing, but one by one, the scribes and Pharisees stole away.

At last, Jesus arose and faced her. "Woman, where are those thine accusers? Hath no man condemned thee?"

Trembling, unable to believe she alone remained before Jesus, she stammered, "No man, Lord."

He looked straight into her eyes. She felt He knew everything about her, more than anyone on earth could know. He spoke. "Neither do I condemn thee: go, and sin no more."

When Jesus had gone, she stood alone in the place where her huddled, broken body would have lain if not for Him, still dazed from the strange encounter with even stranger results. Instead of a death sentence, Jesus had given pardon and an admonition: "Go, and sin no more."

What lay ahead? New life, surely. For once she had looked into Jesus' face and beheld His majesty, the past meant nothing; the future, everything.

RHODA
ACTS 12

Rhoda, who served in the house of Mary the mother of John Mark, made herself small in the corner and listened to the prayers of those around her.

"We beseech Thee on behalf of our brother Peter," one prayed. "Has not Herod, the king, already killed James, the brother of John? Father, Thou knowest how it pleased those Jews who believe not in Jesus so much that Herod further took Peter. Even now our beloved brother lies in prison, guarded by many soldiers. Deliver him, O God, that he may bring us Thy word again."

Rhoda fought back tears. She loved the big, rough man Christ had called from his fishing nets to be a fisher of men. When he laughed, her own lips curved upwards. Most of all, she loved hearing Peter's stories about Jesus.

If only she, too, could have walked with the Master! Rhoda found it hard to stay with her duties when Peter came. She longed to sit at his feet every waking hour. Each retold tale of the Christ made the young maiden's heart beat faster.

She silently prayed for Peter. She knew although it was simple and short, the petition would mingle with the prayers of the others in a mighty plea to God.

Ears made keen by service detected a knocking at the gate. Rhoda's heart gave a sickening lurch. Since Herod had stretched forth his hands to vex certain of the church, believers lived with fear. They refused to give up their beliefs and prayers but knew they, like so many others, might be seized.

On slow feet, the damsel went to the gate. "It is Peter," a voice said.

Relief and joy filled her. So glad was she, Rhoda failed to open the gate, but ran back inside. "Peter even now stands before the gate," she cried.

Disbelief filled their faces. "Thou art mad," they told her.

"Nay," Rhoda insisted again and again. "I did not mistake his voice."

Those in the house looked at one another. "It is his angel."

The knocking increased. At last they opened the door. They gaped in astonishment. Peter stood without, face creased by a broad smile. He beckoned with his hand for them to hold their peace, then stepped inside.

"I have much to tell you," he said in the mighty voice that once bellowed orders to his fishing comrades during wild storms. "This same night I lay sleeping between two soldiers, bound with two chains. The keepers before the door kept the prison." Excitement and triumph shone in his eyes.

"I awakened when a light shined in the prison; I thought it a vision. A man stood before me. He smote me on the side and raised me up, saying, 'Arise up quickly.' My chains clanked; I felt their weight lift when they fell from me.

"The man told me to gird myself and bind on my sandals. He ordered me to cast my garment about me and follow him. I obeyed. When we were safely past the first and the second ward, we came unto the iron gate that leadeth into the city. I marveled, for it opened to us of its own accord. We went out and passed on through one street. My companion departed." He hesitated.

Rhoda felt her body tremble. She had seen Peter in many dispositions, but never had his countenance shone brighter. She clasped her hands and waited.

Peter's voice dropped to a whisper. A look of awe came to his face. "I came to myself and realized where I was. I cried, 'Now I know of a surety, that the Lord hath sent his angel, and hath delivered me out of the hand of Herod, and from all the expectation of the people of the Jews.' I came to this house." His eyes twinkled with merriment. "My young sister grew so excited, she left me standing without the gate."

"In spite of our constant prayers, we did not believe it could really be you," one of the eldest brokenly confessed. "God forgive us! Only this maiden, scarcely past childhood, recognized the truth."

Peter smiled and Rhoda's heart burned within her. She would never forget this night, a night of miracles!

LYDIA
ACTS 16

L ydia of the city of Thyatira was known for her successful selling in the marketplace. Word of her dealings in purple cloth brought to her those from many walks of life. She furnished the finest fabrics to some of the most well-known households in the city, royalty included.

Besides having the high degree of business knowledge needed to compete with other sellers of purple, Lydia possessed an even greater and more precious attribute: she worshipped God.

One Sabbath, she discovered that a much-discussed preacher named Paul intended to pray and speak to the women of the city by a riverside. "I will see for myself what manner of man Paul—once known as Saul, who sought out and persecuted Christians—really is," she told herself.

Seated among the others who flocked to hear, she felt her heart being opened to Paul's message. It burned within her, and when Paul asked for those who believed to come and be baptized, not only she but her entire household came and entered the waters of the river.

Afterwards, she besought Paul, saying, "If ye have judged me to be faithful to the Lord, come into my house, and abide there."

Paul reports, "She constrained us," meaning him and Timothy.

Imagine Lydia's great joy at having them in her home. What stories she and the faithful members of her household must have heard from the determined Paul who now brought people to Christ even more fervently than he had once persecuted them unto death! How many miracles took place within the home she gladly opened to the servant of the Lord? There is no record, but surely the good woman received great blessings in return for her faith and kindness.